FOCUS ON Older People

2005 edition

Editors A Soule, Penny Babb, Maria Evandrou, Stephen Balchin and Linda Zealey

A National Statistics publication

National Statistics are produced to high professional standards
set out in the National Statistics Code of Practice. They are
produced free from political influence.

Contact points

For enquiries about this publication, contact:
Email: focuson.olderpeople@ons.gov.uk

For general enquiries, contact the National Statistics
Customer Contact Centre on: 0845 601 3034
(minicom: 01633 812399)
E-mail: info@statistics.gsi.gov.uk
Fax: 01633 652747
Post: Room 1015, Government Buildings,
Cardiff Road, Newport NP10 8XG

You can also find National Statistics on the Internet at:
www.statistics.gov.uk

About the Office for National Statistics

The Office for National Statistics (ONS) is the government
agency responsible for compiling, analysing and disseminating
economic, social and demographic statistics about the United
Kingdom. It also administers the statutory registration of births,
marriages and deaths in England and Wales. The Director of
ONS is also the National Statistician and the Registrar General
for England and Wales.

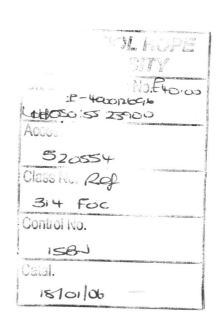

Contents

Page

5: Health and well being

6: Health and social care

7: Economic resources

8: Lifestyles and participation

List of figures and tables

Page

Page

Symbols and conventions

Rounding of figures. In tables where figures have been rounded to the nearest final digit, there may be an apparent discrepancy between the sum of the constituent items and the total as shown.

Billion. This term is used to represent a thousand million.

Provisional and estimated data. Some data for the latest year (and occasionally for earlier years) are provisional or estimated. To keep footnotes to a minimum, these have not been indicated; source departments will be able to advise if revised data are available.

Non-calendar years
Financial year - eg 1 April 2001 to 31 March 2002 would be shown as 2001/02
Academic year - eg September 2000/July 2001 would be shown as 2000/01
Combined years - eg 2000-02 shows data for more than one year that have been combined
Data covering more than one year - eg 1998, 1999 and 2000 would be shown as 1998 to 2000

Units on tables. Where one unit predominates it is shown at the top of the table. All other units are shown against the relevant row or column. Figures are shown in italics when they represent percentages.

Dependent children. Those aged under 16, or single people aged 16 to 18 and in full-time education.

Symbols. The following symbols have been used throughout the report:

..	*not available*
.	*not applicable*
-	*negligible (less than half the final digit shown)*
0	*nil*

List of contributors

Authors:	Stephen Balchin
	Melissa Chan
	Maria Evandrou
	Nina Mill
	Roger Morgan
	Hema Pandya
	A Soule
	Cecilia Tomassini
Production Manager:	Caroline Hall
Production Team:	Liz Attree
	Chris Randall
	Steve Whyman
Review Team:	Catherine Barham
	Hayley Butcher
	Amanda White

Acknowledgements

The editors wish to thank all the authors of individual chapters, and colleagues at the Department for Work and Pensions and the Office for National Statistics who have helped in the preparation of this report.

We are grateful also to our colleagues from the following Departments, devolved administrations and agencies for their generous support and helpful comments:

Office of the Deputy Prime Minister
Department of Health
Department for Transport
Department for Education and Skills
National Assembly for Wales
Northern Ireland Statistics and Research Agency
Scottish Executive
Arts Council England
Institute of Fiscal Studies

Introduction

Focus on Older People is part of the *Focus on* series of publications which combines data from the 2001 Census and other sources to illustrate its topic and provide links to other information. Other reports in the *Focus on* series include analyses of ethnicity, religion, gender, health, the labour market, families, housing, social inequalities and Wales: its people. *Focus on* reports comprise a short overview of the topic area, followed by a more comprehensive analysis in fuller reports. The Overview report for *Focus on Older People* was first published in May 2004 and is now updated and extended with more comprehensive analysis in this publication. Both these reports are now available from the National Statistics website: *www.statistics.gov.uk/focuson*.

This report has been produced mainly in response to an increasing demand for the latest authoritative statistics on issues addressing various aspects about older people's lives, including demographic changes, living arrangements, housing, health, income and lifestyles. Like other *Focus on* publications, this report is aimed at a general audience and presents clear charts and analysis which can be easily understood.

Focus on Older People is the second report on older people published by the Office for National Statistics; the first report entitled *Social Focus on Older People* was published in 1999. This report will provide a resource for all those with an interest in older people's issues, including policy makers, researchers, students and members of the general public.

The report draws on a variety of sources taking into account information presented in several large scale surveys including the General Household Survey, the Labour Force Survey, the Expenditure and Food Survey, the Family Resources Survey and the 2002 English Longitudinal Survey of Ageing. For the purpose of the report, the term 'older people' applies to all those who are aged 50 and over. In certain parts of the report where retirement from work is a key influencing factor, the focus is on people over the state pension age (60 for women and 65 for men). While the aim is to present information for the United Kingdom as a whole, we include some international comparisons and details for parts of the UK.

The report provides references to various data sources in each chapter, as well as suggested further reading which supplements particular topics. We hope the report *Focus on*

Older People is accessible to a wide audience. We also welcome feedback and suggestions for future reports in the *Focus on* series: please email, *focuson.olderpeople@ons.gov.uk*.

Contents and structure of the report

The report is organised into a number of chapters, each concerned with a different aspect of the lives of older people: 1: Demographic profile; 2: Family and living arrangements; 3: Housing; 4: Older people and the labour market; 5: Health and well being; 6: Health and social care; 7: Income, wealth and expenditure; and, 8: Lifestyles and leisure interests.

Chapter 1 (*Demographic profile*) examines the trends and patterns of demographic ageing within the United Kingdom. As birth rates fall, and older people live longer than ever before, the proportion of older people in the population looks set to continue growing. This growth is analysed in terms of sex, geographic distribution, and ethnicity and is compared internationally. The chapter also includes projections of the extent to which the proportion of older people will grow in the future.

Chapter 2 (*Family and living arrangements*) investigates the factors that impact upon the living arrangements of older people. Among the key factors highlighted are marital status, family size, financial well being and health status. These factors will determine whether older people live independently or with others, such as children or in a care home. One notable trend since the end of the Second World War is the increasing proportion of older people living alone, particularly as a result of the rising divorce rate.

Chapter 3 (*Housing*) focuses upon the housing arrangements of older people and how their requirements and preferences change with age. The chapter also shows that older people's housing arrangements are likely to be affected by changes in their health, mobility and marital status. The condition of the houses which older people occupy has a strong impact on their quality of life. This chapter also discusses how certain key indicators of housing standards like overcrowding and under-occupancy affect older people's living arrangements.

Chapter 4 (*Older people and the labour market*) examines the extent and nature of older people's participation in the labour market and looks at the reasons why they do not participate.

The chapter presents information on the different labour market participation rates by age, sex and geographical region. It also looks at the relationship between health and employment. The types of employment of older people are also explored. The focus in this chapter is on the younger end of the over 50s age group.

Chapter 5 (*Health and well being*) investigates issues relating to the health and well being of older people. With the increase in life expectancy and significant declines in adult mortality since the 1950s, older people's expectation of a disability-free life has also increased over the years. This chapter looks at the main causes of death among older people which include diseases of the circulatory system, cancers and diseases of the respiratory and digestive systems. It also looks at the changes older people make in their living habits like giving up smoking in order to adopt healthy lifestyles. The chapter also shows how various factors like housing, socio-economic status and income can contribute to health inequalities in later life.

Chapter 6 (*Health and social care*) explores patterns of use of health and social care services by older people, examining how the use of such services vary with age, sex and health status. Apart from visiting GPs or going to the hospital, older people also make use of various other health services like seeing a dentist or chiropodist. This chapter discusses how frequently they use such services. It also looks into the use of residential care homes by older people, taking into account the use of informal care provided to them by their family members.

Chapter 7 (*Income, wealth and expenditure*) considers the financial resources of older people, of both their incomes and wealth. The level of the financial resources at the disposal of older people is an important contributing factor to the amount of choice and independence that they are able to exercise. This chapter explores the differences in the levels of incomes among particular pensioner groups, that is, women, ethnic minorities and people in the oldest age groups. It also analyses the levels of wealth and savings which people have as they get older, and explains how expenditure patterns change with age.

Chapter 8 (*Lifestyles and leisure interests*) investigates how older people choose to spend their leisure time. As people are living longer than ever before, they now have a greater period of time to pursue the leisure activities they enjoy. This chapter explores which leisure activities they spend most time on, and also looks at some of the barriers, like lack of finance or poor health, which hinder them in pursuing their leisure interests. Older people's lifestyles are also influenced by their desire to participate in society and develop themselves. This chapter also discusses the level of their involvement with clubs, societies, organisations, and with learning new skills.

Demographic profile

Cecilia Tomassini
Office for National Statistics

Key findings

- In 2003 there were 20 million people aged 50 and over in the UK

- Between 1901 and 2003 the proportion of people aged 50 and over in the whole population increased from 15 to 33 per cent and it is projected to be 41 per cent in 2031

- The old population is ageing: people aged 85 and over represented only 1.6 per cent of the 50 and over population in 1951, but represented 5.5 per cent in 2003 and are projected to be 9.1 per cent in 2031

- Women outnumber men at older ages, but the imbalance is projected to decrease in the future

- The UK holds an intermediate position in terms of population ageing within Europe

- There are considerable differences in the proportion of people above state pension age across different areas of the UK

- In 2001 3.5 per cent of the population aged 50 and over were from minority ethnic groups

- A large majority (83 per cent) of older people in England and Wales describe themselves as Christian

Chapter 1

Introduction

Populations are growing older in most of the countries around the world: this trend has characterised the age structure of developed countries for well over a century. Population ageing is defined as the process by which older individuals, in this report people aged 50 or over, make up a proportionally larger share of the total population over a period of time. Demographic ageing relates to the increase in the proportion of older people in the population as a whole and, to a lesser extent, to the increase in the actual number of older people.

Changing UK population over time

Population ageing continues to be an important feature of the UK population. In 1901 nearly one person in seven (15 per cent) was aged 50 and over. This had increased to one in three by 2003 and is still rising. By 2031 it is projected that over 40 per cent of the total population will be aged 50 and over.[1]

The older population is currently growing twice as fast as the population as a whole. The growth rate for the total population was 0.4 per cent between 2002 and 2003, while the rate for people aged 50 and over was 0.8 per cent, and the rate for people aged 65 and over was 0.7 per cent. The UK older population, however, is not increasing as fast as that of some other industrialised countries: in Japan the overall population growth rate was 0.1 per cent compared with a 2.9 per cent increase of the population aged 65 and over between 2002 and 2003.[2]

In the UK, looking at absolute numbers, at the 1901 Census there were 5.7 million people aged 50 and over, representing 14.7 per cent of the total population. By the 2001 Census the number of older people had more than tripled to 19.6 million, comprising 33.3 per cent of the whole population.[3] The population estimates for 2003 show a continuing increase to 20.0 million (Figure 1.1). After 2011 the number of older people is expected to rise again as 'baby-boom' cohorts (born in the late 1950s to late 1960s) reach older ages.[4, 5] Projections by the Government Actuary's Department indicate that the number of people in this age group in the United Kingdom will increase by 36 per cent by 2031, compared with 2003, when the estimated number of people aged 50 and over will be 27.2 million.

A more detailed picture of the age structure of the UK population is given by the analysis of the age pyramids in 1951, 2001 and 2031 (Figure 1.2). The 1951 profile shows:

- a high number of people in the 0–4 age group (due to the baby-boom that occurred in the period 1946–48, immediately after the Second World War);

- a small number of people aged 10–25 (a result of low fertility before and during the Second World War); and

- unbalanced sex ratios above age 55 due to higher male mortality in the First World War.

These features can be traced in the 2001 pyramid where the 50–54 age group is still pronounced (post-Second World War baby boomers), as too are the generations of the 1960s baby-boom (those aged around 30–39). The effects of higher male mortality during the wars can still be seen at very old ages.

In the 2031 pyramid it is still possible to trace the post-war and 1960s baby-boom generations, who by then will be aged 80–84 and 60–69 respectively. These generations of baby boomers have significantly increased the number and the proportions of older people. The population projections illustrated in the 2031 pyramid assume that there will be similar fertility patterns (a stable number of births) to that of 2003 over the next 30 years, but that there will continue to be improvements in survival at older ages. The pyramid is changing shape, becoming more rectangular, with similar numbers of people in each age group.

The absolute number of older people is mainly a result of the number of births five or more decades earlier, and of their subsequent survival. The role of international migration has been far less important in changing the age distribution of the UK than the role of fertility and mortality.[6]

A key factor was the overall decline in fertility that occurred at the end of 19th century and during the 20th century. Falling fertility leads to fewer young people in the population and hence a rise in the proportion of older people. The population aged 0–14 decreased from 12.4 million in 1901 to 10.9 million in 2003, but the share of the total population decreased more dramatically, from 32.5 per cent to 18.3 per cent.[3]

Figure **1.1**

Number of people aged 50 and over

United Kingdom

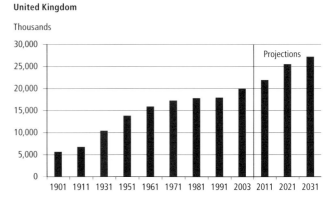

Source: Office for National Statistics; Government Actuary's Department

Figure **1.2**

Population: by age and sex, 1951, 2001 and 2031

United Kingdom

Thousands

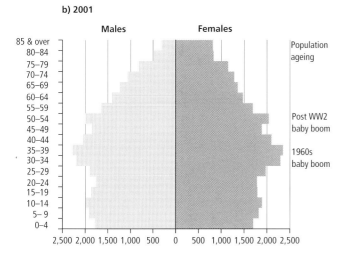

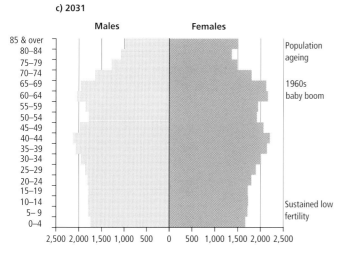

Source: Census, Office for National Statistics; Government Actuary's Department

Declines in mortality rates are also an important factor in the ageing of a population, especially in countries like the UK where fertility levels are already relatively low. Average life expectancy at birth has increased significantly over the last century. In England and Wales, life expectancy at birth in 1901 was 45.0 years for men and 48.8 for women. By 1951 this had increased to 65.7 and 70.7 years respectively. Life expectancy at birth has continued to improve steadily, reaching 76.2 (male) and 80.7 (female) years for 2001–03 in England and Wales.[7]

Much of this improvement, especially in the early part of the 20th century, was a result of a fall in infant mortality. The decline in mortality rates at older ages is, however, particularly important for the ageing of the older population itself. Life expectancy in the UK at age 65 was 13.0 years for men and 16.9 years for women in 1980–82, but had increased to 16.1 and 19.1 years by 2001–03.[7] Thus there has been an upward shift in the proportion of the population at each age range of the 50 and over population (Figure 1.3). In 1951, those aged 50–59 represented 43.0 per cent, and those aged 85 and over made up just 1.6 per cent of the 50 and over population total. In 2003 the two age groups represented 37.8 per cent and 5.5 cent respectively of the older population (even with a slightly reduced cohort for 85 and over because of the 1918 influenza pandemic). Projections indicate these proportions will be respectively 28.2 and 9.1 per cent by 2031.

The median age for the population as a whole rose from 34.1 years in 1971 to 38.4 in 2003 and is projected to rise to 43.3 in 2031. Other developed countries have even higher median ages: Japan, Italy and Germany all have median ages above 40. By 2025, both Italy and Japan project a median age of at least 50.[6] The median age for the UK population aged 50 and over was 64.1 in 2003, but it is projected to rise to 67.1 by 2031.

Figure **1.3**

Age composition of the older population

United Kingdom

Percentages

Source: Office for National Statistics; Government Actuary's Department

3

Improvements in mortality have also occurred after age 80.[8, 9] The remaining life expectancy at age 85 for women born in 1851 in England and Wales was 4.1 years, but it is projected to increase to 8.5 years for women born in 1950.[10] Of 100 women born in 1851, even if they survived to age 85, only one reached her 100th birthday. Of 100 women born in 1951 and surviving to age 85, at least 13 may expect to reach age 100. Therefore an additional indicator for the ageing of the older population is the number of people who are centenarians. In 1911 there were only 100 centenarians in England and Wales.[11] The 2001 Census revealed nearly 8,600 persons aged 100 years old or over (Figure 1.4). This particular age group has the highest growth rate in the whole population, roughly doubling every ten years between 1951 and 2001. The number of centenarians in the United Kingdom is projected to be around 48,000 in 2031, but there is a high level of uncertainty on future trends in mortality at very old ages, with the estimated number of centenarians expected to lie between 30,000 and 72,000.[1]

Because their life expectancy is greater than men's, women outnumber men at the older ages. The ratio of the number of men to the number of women is termed the sex ratio. There were 77 men in the UK aged 50 and over per 100 women of the same age group in 1951. The low sex ratio among older people was partly due to the higher male mortality during the First World War. The sex ratio increased to 85 men per 100 women in 2003, assisted by the recent decline in the mortality rates among men.

Projections indicate that the sex ratio will further increase by 2031, when there are expected to be 90 men per 100 women over age 50. The projected increase in the sex ratio at these ages is mainly a result of the declining gender gap in life expectancy at older ages. More detailed analysis within the 50 and over age group shows a sharp decline in the sex ratio at

the oldest ages. In 2003 there were 98 men for every 100 women among those aged 50–54, but only 40 men per 100 for those aged 85 and over, where probably the effect of the First World War is still present (Figure 1.5). The sex ratio at age 85 and over is estimated to increase considerably by 2031, when there will be 65 men per 100 women.

Regional comparisons across Europe

The UK holds an intermediate position in terms of the ageing of its population within Europe (Table 1.6). European countries 'age' at a different pace, with different fertility and mortality patterns. Between 1960 and 2004 the proportion of people aged 65 and over in the UK increased by around one third, from 11.7 per cent of the total population to 15.6 per cent. In other European countries such as Poland, Portugal, Finland and

Figure 1.5

Sex ratio: by age, 1951, 2003 and 2031

United Kingdom

Number of men per 100 women

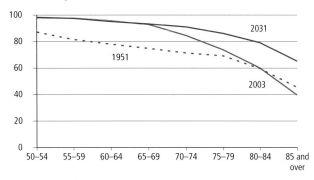

Source: Office for National Statistics; Government Actuary's Department

Table 1.6

People aged 65 and over and 85 and over in selected European countries, 1960 and 2004

Percentages

	65 and over		85 and over	
	1960	2004	1960	2004
Italy	9.3	19.2	0.5	2.0
Germany	11.5	18.0	0.4	1.7
Sweden	11.7	17.2	0.6	2.4
Portugal	7.8	16.7	0.4	1.4
France	11.6	16.4	0.6	1.8
Finland	7.2	15.6	0.3	1.6
United Kingdom	**11.7**	**15.6**	**0.7**	**1.9**
Hungary	8.9	15.5	0.3	1.0
Poland	5.8	13.0	0.3	0.8
Ireland	11.1	11.1	0.6	1.1

Source: Council of Europe; EUROSTAT, New Cronos Database

Figure 1.4

Number of centenarians

England and Wales

Number

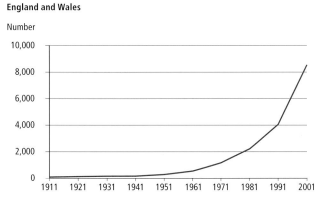

Source: Thatcher (1999) (Reference 12); Census 2001, Office for National Statistics

Figure **1.7**

People aged 65 and over in the European regions, 2003

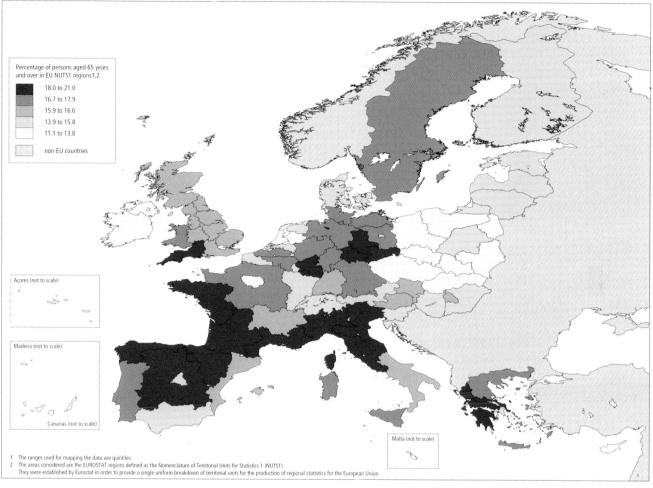

Percentage of persons aged 65 years and over in EU NUTS1 regions1,2

- 18.0 to 21.0
- 16.7 to 17.9
- 15.9 to 16.6
- 13.9 to 15.8
- 11.1 to 13.8
- non-EU countries

Açores (not to scale)

Madeira (not to scale)

Canarias (not to scale)

Malta (not to scale)

1 The ranges used for mapping the data are quintiles.
2 The areas considered are the EUROSTAT regions defined as the Nomenclature of Territorial Units for Statistics 1 (NUTS1).
   They were established by Eurostat in order to provide a single uniform breakdown of territorial units for the production of regional statistics for the European Union.

Source: New Cronos Database, Eurostat

Italy, the proportions of people aged 65 and over more than doubled in the same period, with Poland having the highest increase among the countries considered. In the European Union, Ireland was the only country where the proportion of people aged 65 and over remained constant over this period.

Among the very old population, those aged 85 and over, the increase in the proportion is even more striking: in the UK it increased from 0.7 to 1.9 per cent between 1960 and 2004, but in Finland the proportion of people aged 85 and over increased six fold during the same period. The proportion of very old people in the populations of Sweden, Portugal, Italy and Germany increased by around four fold. Ireland showed the smallest increase where the proportion nearly doubled.

The large increase in the proportion of older people in southern and eastern Europe is due mainly to the rapid and persistent fall in fertility, which has reduced the share of young people in the total population. Additionally, countries in

southern Europe have also experienced rapid improvements in mortality at older ages, which explains the substantial rises in the proportion of people aged 85 and over in those countries. Spain, Italy and France have among the highest life expectancy at age 65 in Europe.[12]

The areas considered in Figure 1.7 are the Eurostat regions defined as the Nomenclature of Territorial Units for Statistics 1 (NUTS1). They were established by Eurostat to provide a single uniform breakdown of territorial units for the production of regional statistics for the European Union.

Looking at the proportion of people aged 65 and over in 2003 at area level in the European Union, Greater London had the seventh lowest proportion (12.1 per cent). Only the Irish Republic, Slovakia, the Canary Islands (Spain), the two Pólnocny regions in Poland, and Cyprus have lower proportions of older people (Figure 1.7). Both higher fertility and high levels of immigration of young people are the main causes for the low proportion of older people in the London region. Conversely, the South West of England has the 14th highest proportion of older people in Europe, with 18.7 per cent aged 65 and over, exceeded only by four German regions, two northern regions and one central region of Italy, three regions in Spain, two regions in southern France and the Central Attic region in Greece.[13] The region with the highest proportion of people aged 65 and over is the north east of Spain, where they account for 21.0 per cent of the total population. Low fertility, emigration of young people and return migration of older people in these areas are the driving forces for the high proportion of older people.

Geographic distribution within the UK

There are clear geographic patterns in the proportions of people above State Pension Age (men aged 65 and over and women aged 60 and over) in the total population across the

different regions of the UK. The areas where the proportion of people above retirement age is higher than 20 per cent are concentrated along the coastal areas of the country, particularly in Cornwall (Figure 1.8). Three local authority districts have over 30 per cent of their population above State Pension Age: Christchurch in Dorset, with 33 per cent; Rother in East Sussex, with 32 per cent; and East Devon, with 30 per cent.[14]

Several factors may explain the substantial differences in the proportion of older people in the UK local authority districts. Many older people choose to leave congested urban areas to settle in coastal and rural locations, while urban and surrounding areas draw younger people for reasons such as studying and greater employment opportunities. Additionally, major cities like London have a higher proportion of people from ethnic minorities, who are characterised by a younger age

Figure **1.8**

People over State Pension Age: by area[1], April 2001

United Kingdom

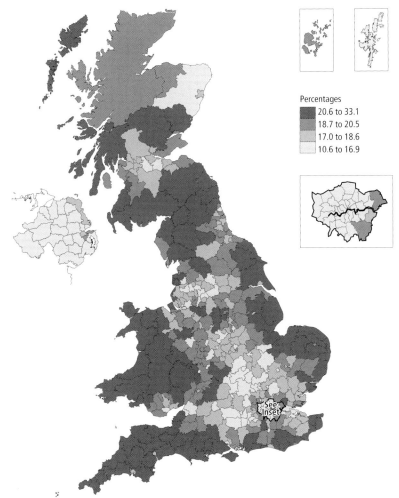

Percentages
- 20.6 to 33.1
- 18.7 to 20.5
- 17.0 to 18.6
- 10.6 to 16.9

1 Unitary and local authorities.

Source: Census 2001, Office for National Statistics; Census 2001, General Register Office for Scotland; Census 2001, Northern Ireland Statistics and Research Agency

structure than the overall population. Northern Ireland has higher fertility than Great Britain, so its age structure is younger than the UK population as a whole.

The growth rate of the population over State Pension Age between 1991 and 2001 is a good illustrator of changes in population age distribution in small areas (Figure 1.9). The local authorities that have seen a decline in the number of older people during this period are urban areas: in particular London (with the exception of Havering, and Kensington and Chelsea), Brighton, Bristol and Glasgow have all seen reductions of more than 10 per cent of their population over State Pension Age. Wandsworth had the greatest loss with a reduction of over 20 per cent. In absolute numbers, Glasgow had almost 13,000 fewer people over State Pension Age in 2001 compared with 1991, and Birmingham 12,000 fewer.

Interestingly, areas in the South East traditionally associated with retirement migration also have a negative growth rate for older people, for example, Worthing, Hastings, Eastbourne and Canterbury. The population over State Pension Age increased by more than 20 per cent in several other areas between 1991 and 2001, for example, Wokingham and Surrey Heath in the South East, and South Staffordshire and Lichfield in the West Midlands. In terms of actual numbers, South Gloucestershire and East Riding of Yorkshire had the largest increases between 1991 and 2001 (almost 8,000 each).

Internal migration is likely to be one of the reasons for the changes in the proportion of people over State Pension Age in different regions. According to the 2001 Census, 4.6 per cent of people aged 50 and over living in England and Wales had changed address in the previous year. Between 1991 and 2001,

Figure **1.9**

Change in population over State Pension Age: by area[1], from 1991 to 2001

Great Britain

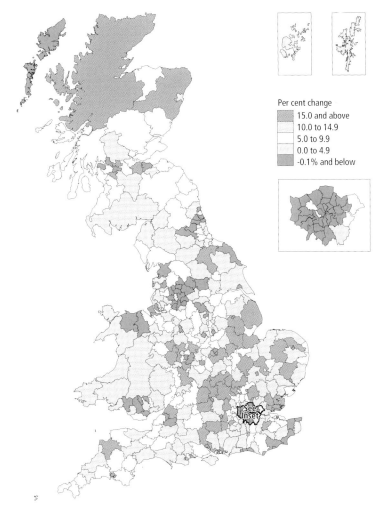

Per cent change
- 15.0 and above
- 10.0 to 14.9
- 5.0 to 9.9
- 0.0 to 4.9
- -0.1% and below

1   *Unitary and local authorities.*

Source: Census 2001, Office for National Statistics; Census 2001, General Register Office for Scotland; Census 2001, Northern Ireland Statistics and Research Agency

© Crown Copyright. All rights reserved (ONS GD272183.2005).

the percentage of men moving in the 12 months before the Census declined from 5.8 to 3.3 per cent between ages 50–54 and 70–74. A similar trend was observed for women, with a slightly higher probability than men to change address after age 70. The percentage moving increased to 8.5 per cent for men aged 90 and over and 10.0 per cent for women (Figure 1.10).

This confirms the general migration pattern for older people approaching retirement ages: a number of people leave urban areas to move to either rural or coastal areas. Beyond State Pension Age the probability of migration is normally low for older people, but tends to increase again when they move to care or nursing homes, or to live with their children or other

Figure **1.10**

People who have changed their address in the last 12 months: by age, 2001

England and Wales

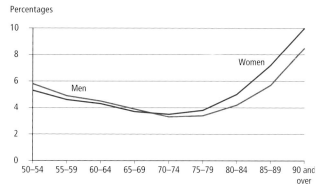

Source: Census 2001, Office for National Statistics

relatives to receive care.[15] However, the absolute number of moves is small at older ages compared with migration occurring at younger ages.

Ethnicity and religion

A very small proportion of older people in Great Britain are from minority ethnic groups. In the 2001 Census 3.5 per cent of the population aged 50 and over were from ethnic minority groups – around 672,000 people – compared with 12.1 per cent of people aged 16 and under (Table 1.11). The percentage falls to 2.5 among those aged 65 and over and to 1.1 per cent for people aged 85 and over – around 13,000 people. The proportions of people aged 65 and older from minority ethnic groups are extremely low in Scotland and Northern Ireland, 0.5 and 0.2 per cent respectively.

There are noticeable differences in the ethnic composition of younger and older generations. These are mainly due to the timing of past migration, the age structure of migrants and past fertility patterns. Immigrants from the Caribbean started to arrive in the UK after the Second World War and through the 1950s and early 1960s. Immigrants from India and Pakistan arrived mainly during the 1960s and early 1970s. Many Asians, mainly of Indian origin, came to the UK from Uganda in 1974. These migration patterns explain the relatively higher proportion of Black Caribbean and Indian older people in the 2001 Census compared with other ethnic groups. In the future, there will be progressive ageing of minority ethnic groups and a higher proportion of older people is projected to be from these groups.[16]

Table **1.11**

Ethnicity: by age, 2001

Great Britain

Percentages

	Under 16	50 and over	85 and over
White	87.9	96.5	98.9
Mixed	2.9	0.3	0.2
Black Caribbean	1.0	0.7	0.2
Black African	1.3	0.2	0.1
Other Black	0.3	0.0	0.0
Indian	2.1	1.1	0.3
Pakistani	2.3	0.5	0.1
Bangladeshi	0.9	0.1	0.0
Other Asian	0.5	0.2	0.1
Chinese or Other	0.8	0.4	0.1
All ethnic groups	100.0	100.0	100.0

Source: Census 2001, Office for National Statistics; Census 2001, General Register Office for Scotland

Figure **1.12**

Age distribution: by ethnic group, April 2001

Great Britain

Percentages

Source: Census 2001, Office for National Statistics; Census 2001, General Register Office for Scotland

Table **1.13**

Older people: by religion[1], 2001

England and Wales   Percentages

	All ages	50 and over		
		Men	Women	All
Christian	71.7	80.1	85.2	82.9
Buddhist	0.3	0.2	0.2	0.2
Hindu	1.1	0.7	0.6	0.7
Muslim	3.0	1.2	0.9	1.0
Sikh	0.6	0.4	0.3	0.3
Jewish	0.5	0.6	0.6	0.6
Other	0.3	0.3	0.2	0.3
Not stated	7.7	7.3	7.4	7.3
No religion	14.8	9.2	4.6	6.7
Total	100.0	100.0	100.0	100.0

1 The data for Scotland and Northern Ireland are excluded as different questions were asked in the 2001 Census.

Source: Census 2001, Office for National Statistics

A closer analysis of the age structure of the ethnic groups in Great Britain reveals that the White Irish have the highest proportion of people aged 65 and over (25 per cent of the total White Irish population in the 2001 Census). The lowest proportion can be found among the Black Africans with only 2.3 per cent of people aged 65 and over (Figure 1.12). Of the non-White ethnic groups, the Black Caribbean group shows the highest proportion of older people (11 per cent).

More people aged 50 and over considered themselves to be Christian than in the overall population of England and Wales, 82.9 per cent compared with 71.7 per cent (Table 1.13). Only 6.7 per cent of people aged 50 and over declared no religion at all, compared with 14.8 per cent of the total population. While 3.0 per cent of the whole population described themselves as Muslims, only 1.0 per cent of people aged 50 and over did so. The proportion of Christians was higher among older women than among men of the same age, while reporting of 'no religion' was higher among men. Differences in the ethnic composition of the older population and migration patterns are probably behind the higher proportion of older men than older women who described themselves as Muslim.

References

1   Government Actuary's Department (2004) Projected populations at mid-years by age last birthday in five-year age group, http://www.gad.gov.uk/Population/2004/uk/wuk025y.xls

2   Statistics Japan (2004) *Population estimates*, http://www.stat.go.jp/english/data/jinsui/2.htm

3   Office for National Statistics (2004) *Annual Abstract of Statistics 2004*, TSO: London.

4   Evandrou M and Falkingham J (2000) Looking back to look forward: lessons from four birth cohorts for ageing in the 21st Century. *Population Trends* **99**, 27–36.

5   Evandrou M (ed) (1997) *Baby Boomers: Ageing in the 21st Century.* Age Concern: London England.

6   United Nations (2002) *World Population Ageing 1950–2050*, Department of Economic and Social Affairs Population Division, United Nations: New York.

7   Government Actuary's Department (2004) *Interim Life Tables*, http://www.gad.gov.uk/Life_Tables/Interim_life_tables.htm

8   Wilmoth J (2000) Demography of longevity: past, present, and future trends. *Experimental Gerontology* **35**, 1111–1129.

9   Vaupel J W, Carey J R, Christensen K, Johnson T E, Yashin AI, Holm N V *et al* (1998) Biodemographic trajectories of longevity. *Science* **280**, **5365**, 855–860.

10   Tomassini C (2005) The demographic characteristics of the oldest old in the United Kingdom. *Population Trends* **120**.

11   Thatcher R (1999) The demography of centenarians in England and Wales. *Population Trends* **96**, 5–12.

12   Council of Europe (2004) *Recent Demographic Developments in Europe*, Strasbourg.

13   New Cronos, Eurostat, http:/europa.eu.int/newcronos/

14   Office for National Statistics (2004) *Focus on Older People* overview http://www.statistics.gov.uk/focuson/olderpeople/default.asp

15   Litwak E and Longino C F (1987) Migration patterns among the elderly: a developmental perspective. *The Gerontologist* **27**, **3**, 266–272.

16   Evandrou M (2000) Social inequalities in later life: the socio-economic position of older people from ethnic minority groups in Britain. *Population Trends* **101**, 32–39.

Further reading

Office for National Statistics (1999) Social *Focus on Older People*, TSO: London.

Office for National Statistics (2004) *Focus on Older People* overview http://www.statistics.gov.uk/focuson/olderpeople/default.asp

Family and living arrangements

Cecilia Tomassini

Office for National Statistics

Chapter 2

Key findings

- Older men are more likely to be married than older women, especially at very old ages

- Older women were twice as likely as men to live alone in 2002: 60 per cent of women aged 75 and over lived alone compared with 29 per cent of men of the same age

- Older Asian people (including Indian, Pakistani, Bangladeshi, Chinese and other Asian groups) are less likely to live alone than older people from White, Black and Mixed ethnic groups

- In 2001 in Great Britain, 4.5 per cent of people aged 65 and over and 20.4 per cent of people aged 85 and over were living in communal establishments. Women are more likely than men to live in communal establishments

- In England in 2001 the overall proportion of people aged 50 and over with living children was 86 per cent for men and 88 per cent for women. Additionally 58 per cent of fathers and 64 per cent of mothers aged 50 or over met with their children at least weekly

- In England in 2001 61 per cent of grandparents aged 50 and over saw their grandchildren at least once a week

Introduction

Population ageing has led to growing interest in family support and interactions. One way to examine family support is to study the living arrangements of older people. Consequently these have attracted great interest among demographers and sociologists as well as among policy makers. Living arrangements are affected by several factors including marital status, family size and structure, financial well being, and health status.[1] Additionally, living arrangements are also affected on the one hand by cultural attitudes (for example, on the value attributed to residential independence) and on the other by the availability of social services for older people. All these factors determine the choices between living independently or with other people (mainly spouse and children): living arrangements are therefore a possible indicator of the availability of potential carers and family support for older people. Additionally, living arrangements may be related to some personal spheres of life of older people: life satisfaction, loneliness, social exclusion and the probability of being institutionalised. This chapter investigates the trends in the family and living arrangements of older people, and the trends in the determinants usually associated with living arrangements such as demographic and attitudinal factors.

Marital status

Spouse availability is clearly a key factor for living arrangements. The current composition by marital status of older people is determined in large measure by past marriage patterns and the incidence and duration of widowhood and divorce. High proportions of cohorts born at the beginning of the last century never married, especially among women due to higher mortality and emigration among men. These patterns explain the high proportion (10 per cent) of never-married women among those aged 85 and over in 2001 (Table 2.1).

Older men are more likely to be married than older women, especially at very old ages. The tendency for men to marry a younger woman and the higher life expectancy of women are the major reasons behind this greater proportion of married men. In 2001 among men aged 60–74, almost four in five were married, compared with three in five women in the same age group. Being married at older ages is an important issue as the spouse is usually the primary source of care. Among men aged 85 and over, 45 per cent are still married compared with 9 per cent of women. The proportion of very old people still married has increased since 1971 when it was 35 per cent for men and 7 per cent for women because of the increase in

survival for both sexes.[2] The proportion of widows increases with age: only 6 per cent of women aged 50–59 are widowed compared with 79 per cent of those aged 85 and over.

Another important feature that also characterises the changes in the marital status of older people is the growing proportion of the divorced population. Between 1971 and 2001 the proportion of divorced people aged 50–59 increased from 1 to 12 per cent for men and from 2 to 14 per cent for women.[2] This increase was partly the effect of the *Divorce Reform Act 1969* in England and Wales, which came into effect in 1971.[3] Higher divorce rates also lead to a higher proportion of people in second or subsequent marriages. In 2001, among married people aged 50 and over, remarried persons represented 16 per cent of the total for men and 14 per cent for women.

Living arrangements

The most important change in the living arrangements of older people in the post-Second World War period was the large increase in the proportion living alone. Dramatic increases in the proportions of older people living alone and decreases in the extent of multi-generational households have been documented in the UK, in many European countries and in the US.[4] There is, however, considerable diversity among European countries in the living arrangements of older people with, in general, much higher proportions of older people living alone in northern than in southern Europe. The propensity to live alone increased between the 1970s and 1990s and then stabilised between the 1990s and 2000s, but the rankings between countries remained largely stable with higher proportions in Sweden and Germany and lower proportions for Italy (Figure 2.2). In Great Britain 34 per cent of non-institutionalised women aged 65 and over were living alone in 1971 compared with 46 in 2001. In Italy the proportion of women aged 65 and over living alone was 22 per cent in 1971 against 36 per cent in 2000. In Sweden the proportion showed a small rise from 47 per cent to 51 per cent during the same period.

Greater financial independence, possible improvements in health, but also rises in the prevalence of divorce and attitudes towards living in communal establishments could be responsible for the increase in independent living for older people, even if these factors may have played different roles among the countries considered. The increase in independent living arrangements has led to considerable concern regarding the availability of family support and the possible effects on the provision of public care services for frail older people when the family is not available.

Table **2.1**

Marital status: by sex and age, 2001

United Kingdom   Percentages

	Total	Single (never married)	Married (first marriage)	Re-married	Separated (but still legally married)	Divorced	Widowed
Men							
50–59	100	10	60	14	3	12	2
60–74	100	8	65	11	2	8	8
75–84	100	7	57	8	1	3	24
85 and over	100	7	38	7	1	2	47
50 and over	100	8	61	12	2	9	9
Women							
50–59	100	6	59	13	3	14	6
60–74	100	6	52	7	1	9	25
75–84	100	7	27	4	1	4	58
85 and over	100	10	8	1	0	2	79
50 and over	100	6	47	8	2	9	28

Source: Census 2001, Office for National Statistics; Census 2001, General Register Office for Scotland; Census 2001, Northern Ireland Statistics and Research Agency

Figure **2.2**

Women aged 65 and over living alone in selected European countries, 1970[1] and 2000[1]

Percentages

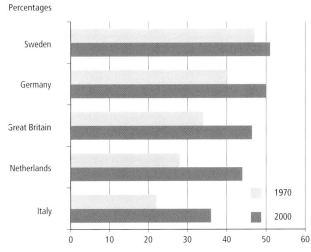

1   Or closest available year.

Source: Tomassini et al (2004) (Reference 4)

In Great Britain, the majority of older men live in a married-couple family: nearly three quarters of men aged 50–59 and around two thirds of men aged 75 and over live with their spouse with or without other family members (Table 2.3 – see overleaf). The proportion of older women living in a married-couple family decreases with age: from seven in ten for women aged 50–59 to three in ten aged 75 and over.

Women are more likely than men to live alone, especially at older ages. Older women were twice as likely as men to live alone in 2002: 60 per cent of women aged 75 and over compared with 29 per cent of men of the same age.

Living without a spouse and with other people (children or other relatives) at older ages is not very common in Britain: only 5 per cent of men and 8 per cent of women aged 75 and over were living with others. Cohabitation is becoming more common among 'young' older people: 5 per cent of men and 4 per cent of women aged 50–59 were living with a partner without being married in 2002.

There are interesting differences among different ethnic groups in terms of living arrangements. Older Asian people (including Indian, Pakistani, Bangladeshi and other Asian groups) are less likely to live alone: while among White men aged 85 and over

Table **2.3**

Older people in households: by sex, age and living arrangements, 2002

Great Britain

Percentages

	Men				Women			
	50–59	60–74	75 and over	Total	50–59	60–74	75 and over	Total
Living alone	15	16	29	18	15	29	60	32
Married couple	73	76	64	73	71	62	31	58
Cohabiting couple	5	3	1	3	4	1	1	2
Without a spouse and with children	4	2	2	3	6	4	5	5
With others	3	3	3	3	3	3	3	3
Total	100	100	100	100	100	100	100	100

Source: General Household Survey, Office for National Statistics

the proportion living alone was 42 per cent, it was only 16 per cent among Asians and 23 per cent among the Chinese or Other group (Figure 2.4). For women in the same age group, the percentages are 71, 22 and 40 respectively. If we consider arrangements different from independent living or as a couple only (here defined as complex household), 12 per cent of White men aged 85 and over lived in a complex household in 2001, compared with 42 per cent of Asians and 29 per cent of the Chinese or Other ethnic group. The differences are even more striking for women: among White women aged 85 and over only 19 per cent lived in a complex household, compared

with 68 per cent among Asian women and 47 per cent of the women in the Chinese or Other groups of the same age. It has been found that South Asian elders are more likely to live in multi-generational households compared with White, Irish and Blacks.[5] Living in complex households has important implications for the provision of care for older people and the risk of institutionalisation, since older people co-residing with relatives can receive informal support at home.

Living arrangements of older people may be also related to their health status. For example, people with limiting long-term

Figure **2.4**

Older people living alone: by sex, age and ethnic group, 2001

United Kingdom

Percentages

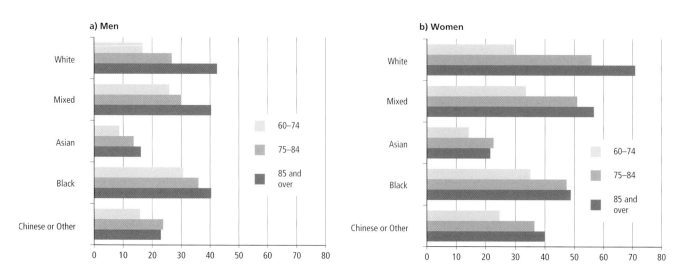

Source: Census 2001, Office for National Statistics; Census 2001, General Register Office for Scotland; Census 2001, Northern Ireland Statistics and Research Agency

illness are less capable of living independently and are more likely to live with other people.[6] In fact among women aged 85 and over with a limiting long-term illness more than 20 per cent were living with other people in 2001 compared with nearly 15 per cent of those with no such illness (Figure 2.5). For men the percentages were 12 and 10 respectively. It is also worth noting that among very old people living alone, 72 per cent reported having a limiting long-term illness at the time of the Census. This group is more likely to be in need of formal or informal care.

Communal establishments

Trends in the proportion of older people in communal establishments are related to several factors. Age, sex and marital status structure of the older population, presence of chronic diseases and disability, and availability of kin all affect the probability of entering an institution. Additionally, changes in legislation regarding the provision of public or private institutional care also play a significant role.

In 2001 in Great Britain, 4.5 per cent of people aged 65 and over were living in communal establishments, a slightly smaller proportion compared with the 5.1 per cent who were doing so in 1991. The reduction in the proportion living in communal

establishments was greater among people aged 85 and over, with 20.1 per cent in 2001 compared with 23.4 per cent in 1991. Women are more likely to live in institutions in old age: among women aged 65 and over, 5.9 per cent were living in communal establishments, compared with just 2.7 per cent of men in the same age group. The percentage of older people in communal establishments increases with age: only 1.1 per cent of both men and women aged 65–74 were living in communal establishments in 2001, compared with 19.7 and 34.2 per cent respectively of men and women aged 90 and over (Figure 2.6). The small fall in the proportion of older people in institutions during the 1990s was, in part, a consequence of the policy response to the expansion in the use of long-term care facilities during the 1980s. New legislation implemented in 1993 (the *1990 NHS and Community Care Act*) was intended to reaffirm the objective of allowing older people to remain in their own homes for as long as possible.[7]

An important factor for the greater presence of women in communal establishments is the different marital status composition: women are more likely to be widowed and so without a spouse to care for them. Another important factor is the higher level of disability reported by women than men at any given older age (see Chapter 5: Health for more information).

Figure **2.5**

People aged 75 and over living in a complex household[1]: by sex, age and presence of limiting long-term illness, 2001

United Kingdom

Percentages

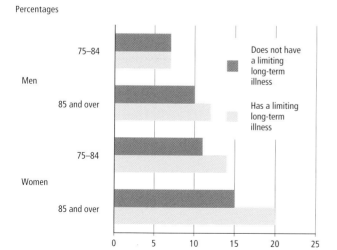

1 A complex household is a household not comprising people living alone or in a couple only.

Source: Census 2001, Office for National Statistics; Census 2001, General Register Office for Scotland; Census 2001, Northern Ireland Statistics

Figure **2.6**

People aged 65 and over in communal establishments: by sex and age, 1991 and 2001

Great Britain

Percentages

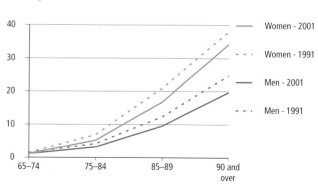

Source: Census 1991 and Census 2001, Office for National Statistics; Census 1991 and Census 2001, General Register Office for Scotland

Figure **2.7**

Marital status composition for all people and those living in communal establishments (CE), aged 65 and over: by sex, 2001

United Kingdom

Percentages

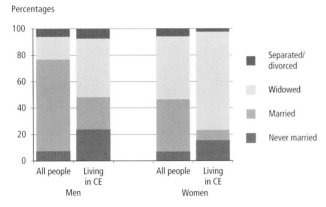

Source: Census 2001, Office for National Statistics; Census 2001, General Register Office for Scotland; Census 2001, Northern Ireland Statistics and Research Agency

Figure 2.7 shows the marital status composition of all people aged 65 and over and those living in communal establishments of the same age in the United Kingdom. The percentage of married older men is 69 per cent in total and only 24 per cent in communal establishments; for older women the percentages are 39 and 8 per cent respectively. Never-married older people are more likely to live in institutions due to the lack of a spouse who could care for them and the high level of childlessness among them. Never-married men represented 24 per cent of

Figure **2.8**

People aged 85 and over living in communal establishments: by ethnic group, 2001

England and Wales

Percentages

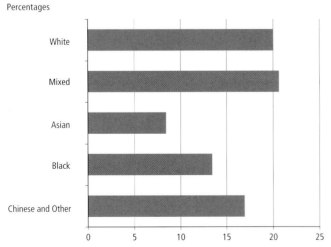

Source: Census 2001, Office for National Statistics

the population in communal establishments against only 7 per cent of all older men; for never-married women the percentages are 16 and 7 respectively.

Ethnic groups are present in different proportions among the older population resident in communal establishments. Figure 2.8 shows that people aged 85 and over from ethnic minorities are less likely to reside in institutions compared with the White and Mixed ethnic groups. In 2001 around 20 per cent of the White and the Mixed population aged 85 and over resided in communal establishments against only 8 per cent and 13 per cent of Asian and Black population respectively. These differences are likely to be related to the tendency of the Asian groups to live in extended families, as noted above.

It is interesting also to examine attitudes towards communal establishments among both younger and older generations. Recent data from a European survey asked adult children about their attitudes towards co-residence and proximity to their own elderly parents who are no longer able to manage alone. Among Britons younger than 40, around 30 per cent would prefer that the parent move to their or to their siblings' home; 13 per cent would move to be close to their parents; and nearly 13 per cent would prefer that their parent moves to a nursing home (Table 2.9). Almost a quarter of British respondents thought that parents should stay at home and receive care there. The percentages were similar when Britons aged 40–64 were considered.

There are considerable differences among different European countries in the attitudes of people towards communal establishments. Children younger than 40 in Southern European countries would consider co-residence to be their favoured option when their parents are no longer able to manage on their own, and they are less likely to opt for a nursing home. In Italy only 2 per cent of people younger than 40 would consider a nursing home as a solution for their frail elderly parents, while more than 52 per cent of them would prefer to have the parent living in their or a sibling's house. It is important to stress though that attitudes may reflect both cultural norms regarding filial responsibility and variations in the availability, cost and quality of institutional care. Among northern European countries the situation is quite different: among Swedish people under age 40, 31 per cent of them think that their parents should move to a nursing home and the proportion increases to 43 for people aged 40–64. Additionally, around 40 per cent of the Swedish respondents think that their parents should stay at home and receive visits there as well as appropriate health care and services, against only 13 per cent of their Portuguese counterparts.

Table **2.9**

People younger than 40 by their opinion on living arrangements for their parents when they become frail[1], selected European countries, 1998

Percentages

	Parent should move to a child's house	A child should move to the parent's house	One should move closer to the other	Parent should move to nursing home	Parent should stay at home, and receive visits	It depends/ Don't know
Sweden	11.4	1.2	7.5	31.1	40.1	8.7
Netherlands	15.9	2.0	7.8	27.5	38.1	8.7
Great Britain	30.5	4.6	13.0	12.6	23.6	15.7
Germany	30.8	6.4	15.7	11.4	22.3	13.4
Italy	51.8	3.0	10.1	2.1	20.9	12.2
Portugal	63.3	2.5	3.2	10.2	12.5	8.3

1 The question in the Eurobarometer survey was: "Let's suppose you had an elderly parent who lived alone. What do you think would be best if this parent could no longer manage to live on his/her own?"

Source: 1998 Eurobarometer 50.1, Eurobarometer Survey Series

Table **2.10**

Opinion of older people on living arrangements for themselves when they become frail: by sex and age, 1997

Great Britain

Percentages

	Men		Women	
	65–74	75 and over	65–74	75 and over
Relatives in your own home	10	22	13	19
Relatives at their home	3	1	0	5
Professional in own home	25	20	29	28
In a nursing or residential home	13	21	11	15
Mix of family and professionals	43	33	41	25
Other[1]	6	3	6	8
Total	100	100	100	100

1 Other includes 'don't know' and 'already required care.'

Source: Omnibus Survey, Office for National Statistics

When attitudes of older people towards care arrangements for themselves in the event that they became dependent were examined, using data from the 1997 National Statistics Omnibus Survey, it was found that 13 per cent of men and 11 per cent of women aged 65–74 would prefer to be looked after in a nursing home (Table 2.10). The percentages were respectively 21 and 15 per cent for men and women aged 75 and over. The proportion of older people who would prefer to be looked after in a nursing home is actually higher than the proportion of older people residing in a nursing home. The favoured option for both older men and women is to receive care from both relatives and professionals.

Number of living children

Kin availability is a key factor in both living arrangement decisions and in care provision for older people. Many studies have shown a positive association between fertility and living in multi-generational households, in the receipt of care and in other dimensions of family support.[8] Older individuals with many children are less likely to live alone than those with few children. In England and Wales, cohorts born in the 1920s are characterised by higher levels of childlessness when compared with the generations born in the mid-1930s and 1940s.[4] Lower fertility among the 'older' elderly cohorts may have contributed, for example, to the low levels of intergenerational co-residence with children observed in England and Wales in the past.

17

Figure **2.11**

Childless older people: by sex and age, 2002

England

Percentages

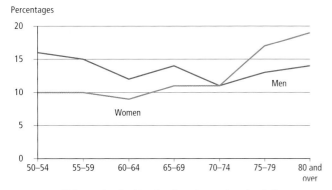

Source: English Longitudinal Study of Ageing, University College London

Figure **2.12**

Older people with two or more children: by sex and age, 2002

England

Percentages

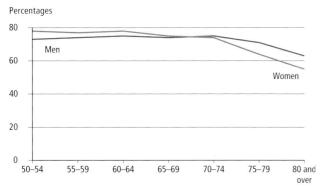

Source: English Longitudinal Study of Ageing, University College London

Figure **2.13**

Older people with step-children: by sex and age, 2002

England

Percentages

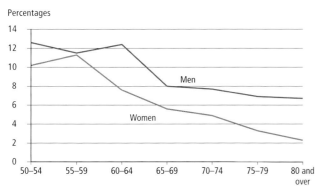

Source: English Longitudinal Study of Ageing, University College London

Data on the number of living children or ever-born children for older people are not often collected in British surveys. Recently the English Longitudinal Study on Ageing (ELSA) filled this gap in information showing some interesting patterns in availability of children for older people.[9] The overall percentage of people aged 50 and over with no living children was 14 for men and 12 for women. There were significant differences in the proportion childless by age (Figure 2.11): very old people are characterised by a high proportion of childlessness (14 per cent of men and 19 of women had no living children at age 80 and over). Older generations are also characterised by a low proportion having two children or more (Figure 2.12): only 55 per cent of women aged 80 and over had more than two children against 78 per cent of women aged 50–54. Younger elderly cohorts today are generally advantaged in terms of availability of at least one child compared with their predecessors born early in the twentieth century: it follows that in the future very old people are more likely to have children that could care for them compared with the earlier generations of people aged 80 and over.[10]

A consequence of high divorce rates is that more older people have stepchildren (Figure 2.13). Overall, 10 per cent of older men had stepchildren, with a higher proportion for those aged 50–54 (13 per cent) and a lower proportion for those aged 80 and over (7 per cent). The same pattern occurred for women: 10 per cent for those aged 50–54 and 2 per cent for those aged 80 and over. The proportion of older people with adopted children was 3 per cent for men and 2 per cent for women.[9]

Contacts with children

Another indicator measuring both the social integration of older people and family resources (in case of need of care) is contact with children. Data on contact and support exchanges between older parents and non co-resident children are sparser than data on household composition. Using data from ELSA, results suggest that intergenerational contact is high: 58 per cent of men and 64 per cent of women aged 50 or over meet with their children at least weekly (Table 2.14). Additionally, 82 and 91 per cent of older men and women report speaking on the phone with their children at least once a week. There is a gender dimension to family contact with, in general, higher levels of contact between mothers and children than between fathers and children. This has been found in many previous studies, suggesting that women maintain greater contact with the family network. There are no significant differences in contact with children by age of parent.

Table **2.14**

Older people by contacts with children[1]: by sex and age, 2002

England

Percentages

	50–59	60–74	75 and over	Total
Men				
Met up with children at least once a week	57	59	55	58
Speak on phone at least once a week	80	84	83	82
Women				
Met up with children at least once a week	65	64	63	64
Speak on phone at least once a week	92	91	90	91

1 Those without grandchildren were excluded.

Source: English Longitudinal Study of Ageing, University College London

Figure **2.15**

Older people who have living grandchildren: by sex and age, 2002

England

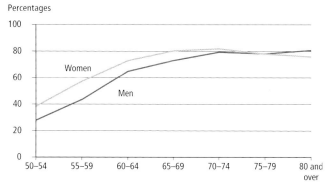

Percentages

Source: English Longitudinal Study of Ageing, University College London

Table **2.16**

People aged 50 and over: by contacts[1] with grandchildren, 2001

Great Britain

Percentages

At least once a week	61
At least every month	17
Only once every three months	10
Less often	11
Never	2
All	100

1 Those without grandchildren were excluded.

Source: Omnibus Survey, Office for National Statistics

A study using data from three British surveys conducted in 1986, 1995 and 1999 examined trends over time in contacts between adult children aged 22–54 and their parents; there was no indication of a trend toward reduced contact.[11]

Grandparenting

A characteristic family role for older people is grandparenting. The availability of grandchildren is both a function of age and number of children. Figure 2.15 shows the proportion of people aged 50 and over in England with living grandchildren. The percentage of men with grandchildren increased from 28 per cent among those aged 50–54 to 81 per cent among those older than 80. For women the percentages are 38 and 76 respectively.

Grandparents often provide day care for their grandchildren when the grandchildren's parents are working or studying. A recent study conducted by Age Concern England found that one in four grandparents care for their grandchildren on a regular basis.[12] The National Statistics Omnibus Survey also reported that 60 per cent of grandparents looked after grandchildren when they were younger than 15.[13]

Grandparents also have very frequent contact with their grandchildren. Among those with grandchildren not living with them, 61 per cent see them at least once a week and an additional 17 per cent at least once a month (Table 2.16). Only a small proportion of grandparents (2 per cent) has no contact with grandchildren. There are no significant differences between men and women in the frequencies of having contact with grandchildren. Grandfathers were less likely to meet grandchildren when they were not living with their wives.[13]

References

1   United Nations (2001) *Living Arrangements of Older Persons, Population Bulletin of the United Nations*, Special Issue 42/43/ 2001.

2   Office for National Statistics (1991) *Census Historical Tables: Great Britain*, (Table 5). Northern Ireland General Register Office (1971) *Census of Population 1971 Summary Tables*, (Table 5) Belfast.

3   Haskey J (1986) Recent trends in divorce in England and Wales: the effects of legislative changes, *Population Trends* **44**, 9–16.

4   Tomassini C, Glaser K, Wolf D, Broese van Groenou M and Grundy E (2004) Living arrangements among older people: an overview of trends in Europe and the USA. *Population Trends* **115**, 24–34.

5   Evandrou M (2000) Social inequalities in later life: the socio-economic position of older people from ethnic minority groups in Britain. *Population Trends* **101**, 32–39.

6   Glaser K, Murphy M and Grundy E (1997). Limiting long-term illness and household structure among people aged 45 and over, Great Britain 1991. *Ageing and Society* **17**, 3–19.

7   Grundy E and Glaser K (1997) Trends in, and transitions to, institutional residence among older people in England and Wales, 1971–91. *Journal of Epidemiology and Community Health* **51**, 531–540.

8   Wolf D A (1994) The elderly and their kin: Patterns of availability and access, in Martin L G and SH Preston S H (eds) *Demography of ageing*, Academy Press: Washington D C, 146–194.

9   Marmot M, Banks J, Blundell T, Lessof C and Nazroo J (eds) (2003) *Health, wealth and lifestyle of the older population in England - English Longitudinal Study of Ageing 2002*, The Institute of Fiscal Studies: London.

10   Murphy M and Grundy E (2003) Mothers with living children and children with living mothers: the role of fertility and mortality in the period 1911–2050. *Population Trends* **112**, 36–44.

11   Grundy E and Shelton N (2001) Contact between adult children and their parents in Great Britain 1986–1999. *Environment and Planning* **33**, 685–697.

12   Age Concern England website. http://www.ageconcern.org.uk/ ageconcern/staying 1158.htm

13   Clarke L and Roberts C (2003) Grandparenthood: its meaning and its contribution to older people's lives. *Growing Older Programme*, Research Finding 22.

Housing

Hema Pandya[1], Melissa Chan[1], Nina Mill[2]
[1] Office of the Deputy Prime Minister,
[2] Office for National Statistics

Key findings

- Three quarters of older households in Great Britain (where the head was aged 50 and over) were owner occupiers in 2003/04: 52 per cent owned their homes outright and an additional 23 per cent were buying their home with a mortgage

- Widowed, married and single older households were most likely to live in owner-occupied accommodation that was owned outright. Older divorced or separated households were most likely to live in property rented from the social sector

- In 2001 a third of older households lived in non-decent housing. Homes rented privately were most likely to be non-decent (54 per cent). Among owner occupiers, households headed by someone aged 85 and over were almost twice as likely as those aged 50–64 to live in non-decent housing

- Over half a million older people were estimated to be living in sheltered accommodation in 2003/04, a rise of over 75 per cent since 1994/95. In 2003/04, 43 per cent of those in sheltered accommodation were council tenants and 40 per cent were with registered social landlords

- In 2001, 424,000 older people in England and Wales lived in communal establishments - almost half were aged 85 and over. Women living in communal establishments (particularly the widowed and never-married) far outnumbered male residents (303,000 women compared with 121,000 men)

Chapter 3

Introduction

As people progress through life and their family structures and financial situations change, so do their housing requirements and preferences. This chapter provides information about the housing patterns and characteristics of older households (generally those aged 50 and over) living in private households and communal establishments.

Housing characteristics

Three quarters of households in Great Britain where the head was aged 50 and over were owner occupiers in 2003/04: 52 per cent owned their home outright and an additional 23 per cent were buying their home with a mortgage (Table 3.1). One in five households lived in social housing, rented from the local authority or housing association and one in twenty were rented privately. Households containing older people aged 65 and over were more likely than other households to own their own home outright (66 per cent of those aged to 65–84 and 61 per cent of those aged 85 and over compared with 39 per cent of households where the head was aged 50–64). Households in the younger age group (aged 50–64) were more likely to be buying with a mortgage reflecting the fact that many people pay off their home loans as they approach retirement. The proportion of households living in social rented accommodation increased with age. Among those aged 50–64, 15 per cent were social renters. This compared with 24 per cent of people aged 65–84, and 29 per cent of those aged 85 and over.

The type of housing people live in, and particularly whether they have to negotiate stairs, will have a bearing on how well they can get about at home. Over four fifths of older households lived in a house or bungalow in 2003/04 (Table 3.2). However the proportion living in this type of property reduced with age while the proportion living in a flat or maisonette increased. Among households headed by someone aged 50–64, the proportion living in a house or bungalow was 87 per cent. This fell to 71 per cent of households headed by someone aged 85 and over. Conversely 12 per cent of households headed by someone aged 50–64 lived in a flat or maisonette compared with 28 per cent of households headed by someone aged 85 and over. Around one in eight (13 per cent) older households lived in a flat on the first floor or lower and 2 per cent lived in a flat at a higher level with a lift. For a further 1 per cent, their flats were on the second floor or above with no lift, which could limit the freedom of movement for those with restricted mobility.

Marital status also has an impact on older peoples' housing circumstances. Widowed, married and single household heads aged 50 and over were most likely to live in owner-occupied accommodation that was owned outright (60 per cent, 55 per cent and 49 per cent respectively) (Table 3.3). Older divorced or separated household heads were most likely to live in property rented from the social sector. Single and divorced or separated households were least likely to live in a house or bungalow (both 69 per cent) compared with 94 per cent and 76 per cent of married and widowed older households respectively.

Table **3.1**

Tenure: by age of household reference person, 2003/04

Great Britain				Percentages
	50–64	65–84	85 and over	All aged 50 and over
Owner occupied				
Owned outright	39	66	61	52
Buying with mortgage	40	7	2	23
Social rented	15	24	29	20
Private rented	6	4	8	5
All tenures[1]	100	100	100	100

1 Includes accommodation that goes with the job of someone in the household or that is rent free.

Source: General Household Survey, Office for National Statistics

Table **3.2**

Type of dwelling: by age of head of household, 2003/04

Great Britain				Percentages
	50–64	65–84	85 and over	All aged 50 and over
House or bungalow				
Detached	30	26	25	28
Semi-detached	34	33	28	33
Terrace	23	23	17	23
All	87	82	71	84
Flat or maisonette				
Purpose built	11	15	27	14
Conversion	2	1	1	2
All	12	17	28	15
All dwellings[1]	100	100	100	100

1 Includes other types of dwellings.

Source: General Household Survey, Office for National Statistics

Table 3.3

Housing tenure: by marital status

Great Britain   Percentages

	Single	Married	Divorced or Separated	Widowed	All aged 50 or over
Owner occupied,					
Owned outright	49	55	31	60	52
Buying with mortgage	18	30	26	6	23
Social rented	26	11	34	28	20
Private rented	8	4	9	6	5
All tenures	100	100	100	100	100

Source: General Household Survey, Office for National Statistics

Residential mobility tends to decline in later life. In 2003/04 less than one in ten households in Great Britain where the head was aged 50 and over had moved during the previous two years. This compares with around one in five of all households. Almost three quarters of households where the head was aged 50 and over had been living at their property for more than 10 years. As might be expected, the length of time a householder has lived in their home increases with age, for example 39 per cent of householders aged 50–64 had lived in their home for 20 years or more compared with 57 per cent of those aged 85 and over (Table 3.4). These figures, however, exclude older people who moved into communal establishments, as the General Household Survey only covers people resident in private households.

The Survey of English Housing asked respondents in 2003/04 who had moved within three years of the date of their interview about their main or only reason for moving. For those

Table 3.5

Main reason for moving: by pre-move tenure and age of household reference person, 2003/04

England   Percentages

	50–64	65–84	85 and over
To move to a better neighbourhood or more pleasant area	17	14	7
Job related reasons	10	3	0
Wanted larger or better house or flat	12	5	13
Wanted smaller or cheaper house or flat	14	23	27
Could not afford mortgage payments or rent	2	0	0
Divorce or separation	12	3	0
Marriage or began living together	3	2	0
Other family or personal reasons	18	42	54
Wanted to buy	3	1	0
Wanted own home or to live independently	4	2	0
Tenant had to leave	6	5	0
All that moved (=100%) (thousands)	579	294	18
Did not move (thousands)	5,074	4,704	508

Source: Survey of English Housing, Office of the Deputy Prime Minister

in households where the head was aged 50–64 the main reasons for moving included wanting to move to a better neighbourhood or more pleasant area, wanting a smaller or cheaper house or flat, divorce or separation, and 'other' family reasons (which were not identified separately) (Table 3.5). For those aged 65–84 and those 85 and over, 'other' family and personal reasons were the most common response, followed

Table 3.4

Length of residence: by age of household reference person, 2003/04

Great Britain   Percentages

	Length of residence of household reference person							
	Less than 12 months	12 months but less than 2 years	2 years but less than 3 years	3 years but less than 5 years	5 years but less than 10 years	10 years but less than 20 years	20 years or more	Total[1]
50–64	4	4	4	7	14	28	39	100
65–84	2	3	3	5	12	21	54	100
85 and over	3	2	1	3	8	24	57	100

1 Total also includes households where the length of residence is unknown.

Source: General Household Survey, Office for National Statistics

by wanting a smaller or cheaper house or flat. It should be noted that only a very small proportion (3 per cent) of people aged over 85 had moved in the past three years.

Housing conditions

Housing conditions are an important aspect of quality of life. For example, ownership of some durables has been found alongside housing tenure and housing quality to be related to health among older people.[1]

Among the consumer durables that the General Household Survey in Great Britain asks respondents whether they have access to are labour-saving devices, such as washing machines or microwave ovens.[2] These may lighten the load of housework and perhaps enable people to function independently for longer. Items such as fridges and fridge freezers might reduce the number of shopping trips needed. Telephones provide a means of maintaining contact with friends and family. For those who spend a lot of time at home, entertainment items such as televisions and video recorders may enrich quality of life.

Like most households, in 2003/04 high proportions of older households (where the household head was aged 50 and over) had a fridge or fridge-freezer (95 per cent), a washing machine (92 per cent) and a microwave oven (86 per cent) (Table 3.6). Almost all households had a telephone (99 per cent). The availability of entertainment items varied according to the item; nearly all older households had a television (99 per cent) while only 86 per cent had a video recorder/player.

Table **3.6**

Households with central heating and selected consumer durables: by age of household reference person, 2003/04

Great Britain				Percentages
	50–64	65–84	85 and over	All aged 50 and over
Central heating	94	93	89	93
Telephone	99	99	99	99
Television	99	99	100	99
Video recorder/player	93	82	54	86
Microwave oven	91	84	68	86
Washing machine	96	91	73	92
Fridge or fridge freezer	96	94	91	95

Source: General Household Survey, Office for National Statistics

In general access to the consumer durables listed in Table 3.6 declined with household age. For example, whereas over nine in ten households aged 50–64 had a video recorder/player this was the case among just over half of households aged 85 and over. Similarly 91 per cent of households aged 50–64 had a microwave compared with 68 per cent of those aged 85 and over.

Given the consequences of cold winters on the health of older people, of particular interest is the proportion of older households with central heating. Almost all older households had central heating (93 per cent), although slightly fewer households aged 85 and over had it (89 per cent).

Respondents to the English Longitudinal Study of Ageing in 2002 were asked whether their homes had any special features to assist people who had physical impairments or health problems, such as handrails or stair lifts. Almost three fifths of people reported having handrails installed in their accommodation while almost half reported having adapted the bathroom. Generally, those in the older age groups were likely to have more adaptations to their home. This is likely to reflect the decrease in physical ability as people get older.

Important indicators of housing standards are overcrowding and under-occupancy. The bedroom standard measures the number of bedrooms actually available to a household against the number of bedrooms required given the household's size and composition. Although overcrowded accommodation has been found to be associated with mortality, even at older ages, in fact for many older households under-occupation may be an issue and may relate to isolation and loneliness.[1]

'Bedroom Standard' is used as an indicator of occupation density. A standard number of bedrooms are allocated to each household in accordance with its age/sex/marital status composition and the relationship of the members to one another

Generally older households are more likely than all households to live in under-occupied accommodation (that is having two or more rooms above the bedroom standard). In 2003/04 around four fifths of households where the reference person was aged 50 and over lived in under-occupied accommodation compared with a third of all households. For those households where the reference person was aged between 50 and 84, around half had homes that were two rooms or more above the bedroom standard (Table 3.7). This is perhaps to be expected, particularly among widowed people, and those whose children have grown up and left home. Indeed married older households were the most likely to live in houses that were above the bedroom standard (90 per cent) compared

Table 3.7

Bedroom standard: by age of household reference person, 2003/04

Great Britain   Percentages

	One or more below	At standard	One room above	Two or more rooms above
50–64	2	15	34	49
65–84	0	17	33	49
85 and over	0	28	36	37

Source: General Household Survey, Office for National Statistics

with 77 per cent of widowed households, 75 per cent of single households and 69 per cent of divorced or separated households.

The likelihood of being above the bedroom standard has increased over the last 30 years or so, a change which has been apparent among all households. In 1971 around a fifth of households lived in homes that were two or more rooms above the standard. This rose to around a third in 2003/04. In contrast the overall proportion with homes below the bedroom standard fell from 7 per cent to 2 per cent between 1971 and 2003/04.

Another important aspect of older people's housing is the condition of their dwelling. To be considered 'decent' a dwelling must meet the statutory minimum standard for housing (that is be fit); be in a reasonable state of repair; have reasonably modern facilities and services; and provide a

Table 3.8

Non-decent homes[1]: by tenure and age[2], 2001

England   Percentages

	50–64	65–84	85 and over	All aged 50 and over
All owner occupied	28	34	51	31
Social rented	43	36	37	38
Private rented	..	..	..	54
All tenures	32	35	48	34

1 Non-decent homes is an indicator combining unfitness, substantial
   disrepair and where essential modernisation is needed.
2 The base is the number of households headed by an older person
   within the age group.

Source: English House Condition Survey, Office of the Deputy Prime Minister

reasonable degree of thermal comfort. Results from the 2001 English House Condition Survey showed that around a third of households where the household head was aged 50 and over lived in non-decent housing and this proportion increased with age to almost half of those aged 85 and over (Table 3.8). Older households (all aged 50 and over) renting privately were most likely to be living in non-decent homes (54 per cent). Among older households who were owner occupiers, those aged 85 and over were almost twice as likely as those aged 50–64 to live in non-decent housing (51 per cent compared with 28 per cent respectively). However among those renting in the social sector the reverse was true: households where the head was aged 85 and over were less likely than those aged 50–64 to live in non-decent accommodation (37 per cent compared with 43 per cent respectively).

Among all of the older age groups the most common reason for a dwelling to be declared non-decent was the failure to provide a reasonable degree of thermal comfort (Figure 3.9). Almost three in ten older households (aged 50 and over) did not meet the standard for this reason. Among households where the head was aged 85 and over, this proportion rose to 42 per cent. However when asked about their own home in the English Longitudinal Study of Ageing, only a minority of people aged 50 and over reported problems. About 12 per cent of older people said that their house was too cold in winter. One in ten older people complained of damp rising in floors and walls, of problems with insects, mice or rats or the house being too dark.

Figure 3.9

Non-decent homes[1]: by reason for non-decency and age, 2001

England
Percentages

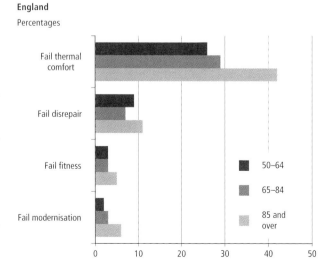

1 Across all tenures.

Source: English House Condition Survey, Office of the Deputy Prime Minister

Housing support

Housing support provided by the government for older people includes sheltered and extra care housing and giving support to those who wish to continue living in their own homes, but need some help to do so.[3] Sheltered accommodation provides a self-contained home which can range in size and layout from a small apartment, to a larger flat with more than one bedroom, or a bungalow. Sheltered housing can also vary in the level and type of facilities offered – ranging from having a scheme manager or warden on-site to being linked to a community alarm system through which help or attention can be summoned. Other features such as communal areas and facilities and safety provisions can also vary. While residents tend to be aged 60 or more, in recent years sheltered housing has also been rented or sold to people in their 50s.

Although sheltered housing has been available since the 1940s, the main developments in this field were in the 1960s and 1970s when sheltered housing was seen as an alternative to residential care.[4] In the 1980s, private developers began providing sheltered housing for sale. Since the mid-1980s, however, the emphasis has switched to enabling people to stay at home for as long as they are able to or wish to do so, with the assistance of home adaptations and repairs, plus home care and support.

In 2000 there were 915 thousand dwellings designed for older people in England, of which nearly 60 per cent were sheltered or very sheltered housing. Local authorities owned 50 per cent of sheltered accommodation; registered social landlords owned 40 per cent; while the remaining 10 per cent were privately owned.

Data from the Survey of English Housing (SEH) showed that between 1994/95 and 2003/04 the number of older people living in sheltered accommodation increased by over 75 per cent to 534,000. However these estimates are probably underestimates as the SEH only asks whether the respondent's accommodation is sheltered housing if all persons in the household are aged 65 or older. In 1994/95, 63 per cent of residents were council tenants, while 21 per cent were tenants of registered social landlords, 14 per cent were owners and 2 per cent private tenants (Figure 3.10). In 2003/04 the proportion of council tenants had declined to 43 per cent, the proportion of tenants of registered social landlords had risen to 40 per cent, while the proportions of owners and private tenants were little changed (16 per cent and 2 per cent respectively).

Another option is extra care housing, a newer form of sheltered housing, offering a greater degree of support and care services. This offers flexible care with 24-hour support

Figure 3.10

Older people in sheltered accommodation: by tenure

England
Percentages

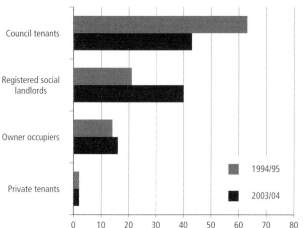

Source: Survey of English Housing, Office of the Deputy Prime Minister

from social care and health teams. It is intended for people who are less able to manage on their own, but who do not need the level of care available in a residential home. The services offered can vary between schemes, but meals and some personal care are usually available.

The other newer support service, which is not dependent on residency in a particular property, or type of property, is called floating support. Many older people who could not previously claim for support (such as owner occupiers) can now get a subsidy for support services. Local authorities are developing new floating support services targeted at older people, or expanding existing floating support services that before only applied to social tenants.

Communal establishments are the traditional form of housing support for older people. In 2001, there were 424,000 older people (aged 50 and over) in England and Wales living in communal establishments of whom almost half were aged 85 and over. Women living in communal establishments far outnumbered male residents (121,000 men compared with 303,000 women) (Figure 3.11) (see Chapter 2: Living arrangements for more information on older people living in communal establishments).

An analysis undertaken by the Centre for Research on Ageing and Gender using 2001 Census data illustrated that gender differences in marital status accounted for much of the variation in communal establishment residence. The widowed and never married are more likely to live in institutional care in later life and these groups are disproportionately women.[5]

Figure **3.11**

People living in communal establishments: by age and sex, 2001

England and Wales

Thousands

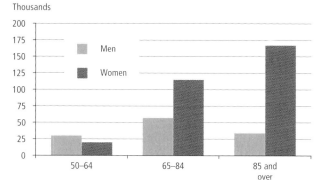

Source: Census 2001, Office for National Statistics

Marital status provides a proxy for the availability of family carers. At all five-year age groups at 65 and above, the never married are most likely to live in a communal setting (nursing, residential or other health care establishment) (Figure 3.12). They are at least five times more likely than the married to be communal residents in each age group below 85. The widowed are between the two extremes (as are the divorced, who are not shown in the figure). Under age 80, the widowed have less than half the level of communal residence of the never married, illustrating the role of adult children in providing care. Under age 85, the widowed are over three times more likely to live in a residential setting than the married, demonstrating the major

role of marital partners in providing care and delaying residential admissions (see Chapter 6: Health and social care for more information).

References

1. Janevic M, Gjonça E & Hyde M. (2003). Physical and social environment. In (eds) M Marmot, J Banks, R Blundell, C Lessof, J Nazroo. *Health, wealth and lifestyles of the older population in England: the 2002 English Longitudinal Study of Ageing.* Institute for Fiscal Studies: London.

2. Office for National Statistics (2001) *People aged 65 and over supplement.* General Household Survey. The Stationery Office: London. http://www.statistics.gov.uk/lib2001/index.html

3. *Supporting People Programme* (2003) Office of the Deputy Prime Minister.http://www.odpm.gov.uk/stellent/groups/odpm_housing/documents/page/odpm_house_602057.hcsp

4. Matheson J & Summerfield C (1999) *Social Focus on Older People.* The Stationery Office: London.

5. Arber S & Ginn J (2004) Ageing and gender: diversity and change. In: C Summerfield and P Babb (eds) *Social Trends 34th edition.* The Stationery Office: London. http://www.statistics.gov.uk/socialtrends

Figure **3.12**

People aged 65 and over living in communal establishments[1]: by age and marital status[2], 2001

England and Wales

Percentages

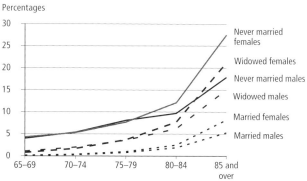

1 *General hospitals, psychiatric hospitals/homes, other hospitals, nursing homes, residential care homes and other medical and care homes and other establishments*
2 *Divorced and separated people have been omitted, in order to show more clearly the differences between married, widowed and never married older people.*

Source: Census 2001, Office for National Statistics (Reference 5)

Older people and the labour market

Roger Morgan

Department for Work and Pensions

Key findings

- Employment rates decline with age from age 50, with only about half of people one year below State Pension Age (SPA) being in work

- Older people in work are more likely than those in work aged 25–49 to be self-employed (one in six of those aged 50-SPA in work) or working part time (a quarter of those aged 50-SPA in work). Among those in work over SPA the majority of both men and women work part time

- Older people who are out of work are more likely to be economically inactive (over nine tenths of those out of work) than available for and actively seeking work. Among the economically inactive aged 50-SPA sickness, injury or disability are more commonly given as reasons for not seeking work than is retirement

- The employment rate of older men in 2004 was substantially lower than that in 1979 (when the data series began). The rise in employment for older women reflects wider social changes, but both men and women who have been economically active seem to depart the labour market earlier than in 1979

- The increase in the employment rates of older people has in recent years exceeded the rise for those aged 25–49

- Over a third of people aged 50–69 who have retired consider that they were forced into retirement. Health problems were the single most common reason given

Chapter 4

Introduction

As people get older their involvement in the labour market changes as they begin to prepare for retirement. This chapter discusses the employment rate of older people, the type of economic activity pursued, and how this activity has changed over time and with age. It also looks at reasons for economic inactivity among older people. Most of the information, which relates to the United Kingdom, is derived from the Labour Force Survey (LFS) and is not seasonally adjusted unless otherwise stated.

Significant changes in the population structure of the United Kingdom have resulted in there being fewer young people and more people aged 50 and over. Falling fertility rates has led to fewer young people in the population and hence a rise in the proportion of older people. In addition, falls in death rates at older ages have contributed to the increase in the number of older people. Projections suggest this trend will continue. In 2004 around 34 per cent of the population was aged 50 and over and it is estimated that this proportion will increase to 40 per cent in 20 years (see Chapter 1: Demographic profile for more details).

Older workers are likely to play an increasingly important role in the labour market. By 2022 there will be an estimated 1 million fewer working-age people under 50 and 3 million more working-age people aged 50 and over. There is also a trend for more young people to stay longer in full-time education and therefore begin full-time work at a later age. If substantial numbers of older people continue to leave the labour market this is likely to have a direct impact on the size of the working population.[1]

Patterns of economic activity

The majority of people aged between 50 and State Pension Age (SPA) in the United Kingdom are in work, 69.9 per cent in spring 2004. Unemployment rates in older people are low: 2.9 per cent of economically active people aged 50 and over were unemployed in spring 2004, compared with the national average of 4.8 per cent. Unlike any other age group unemployment and economic inactivity for those aged 50 and over are more likely to be influenced by the decision of when to retire. Most older people who are not working are not seeking work or are not available to start work, and hence classified as economically inactive. Later sections of this chapter look at the reasons for people being out of work (see the Glossary on page 38 for definitions of economic activity and inactivity).

Employment and unemployment fall across the older age groups (over 50) as economic inactivity increases (Figure 4.1). The employment rate of men aged 25–49 in spring 2004 was 88.2 per cent, compared with 53.4 per cent for the 60–64 age group. In contrast, the economic inactivity rate rose from 8.2 per cent among those aged 25–49 to 44.3 per cent for men aged 60–64, and then to 81.7 per cent for men aged 65–69. The patterns are broadly similar for women.

Participation in the labour market tends to decrease for both men and women from around the age of 50 (Figure 4.2). In 2004 the economic activity rate was 89.9 per cent for men aged 50 and 77.3 per cent for women of the same age in the United Kingdom. The rate fell gradually for both sexes from the early 50s but the rate of decline accelerated for both sexes in their late 50s, with a sharp fall in the years prior to State

Figure **4.1**

Economic activity breakdown: by age group and sex, spring 2004

United Kingdom
Percentages

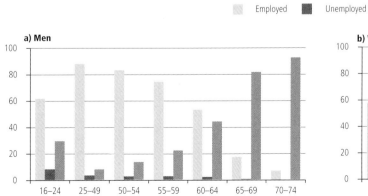

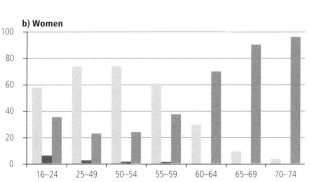

Source: Labour Force Survey, Office for National Statistics

Figure **4.2**

Economic activity rate: by age and sex, spring 2004

United Kingdom

Percentages

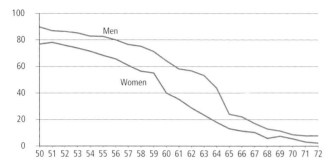

Source: Labour Force Survey, Office for National Statistics

Pension Age. By age 59, 71.3 per cent of men and 55.5 per cent of women were active. For women the rate then fell steeply on reaching SPA so that at age 60, 40.4 per cent were active. For men the decrease in activity levelled off through the early 60s before falling sharply – just over half of men aged up to 63 were employed or looking for work. By age 64, 43.9 per cent of men were active after which the rate then dropped to 24.0 per cent of men aged 65. The Labour Force Survey categorises economically inactive people aged five years or more over SPA as 'retired'. Nearly 8 per cent of men aged 71–72 were economically active in 2004.

Older people in employment

The proportion of older people who were in employment has risen in recent years. In spring 2004, 71.9 per cent of men aged 50–64 were in employment, compared with 17.8 per cent of men aged 65–69 (Figure 4.3). The employment rate for men

Figure **4.3**

Employment in older people: by sex and age[1], 1979 to 2004

Great Britain

Percentages

1 State pension age (SPA) is 60 for women and 65 for men.

Source: Labour Force Survey, Office for National Statistics

over 50 started to recover during the 1990s after years of decline following a sharp fall after 1979 (when LFS data first became available). In 1979, 84.3 per cent of men aged 50–64 and 16.3 per cent of men aged 65–69 were in employment. Evidence from sources other than the LFS suggests that 1979 was not a peak in the employment rate of older men. In the case of men aged 65–69 economic activity seems to have declined between 1951 and 1975.[2]

The increase in employment was shared by both men and women. In spring 2004, 67.9 per cent of women aged 50–59 and 29.8 per cent aged 60–64 were in employment, compared with 56.9 and 20.9 per cent of women in the same age groups in 1979. This increase is likely to be linked to the ageing of birth cohorts of women who had higher employment rates earlier in life than earlier cohorts. For example, around 56 per cent of women born between 1940 and 1949 were in employment at any time when 30 years old compared with around 48 per cent of women born between 1930 and 1939.[3] The OECD has estimated that the average age of withdrawal from the labour force in the United Kingdom fell between the early 1970s and the late 1990s for both men and women.

Despite the rise in employment a large proportion of older people still experience barriers to finding work. The National Audit Office suggested that those who were relatively easy to place had found jobs.[4] An increasing proportion of those remaining out of work are harder to help as they face barriers to employment, such as age discrimination and transport difficulties.

The employment status of the workforce varies with age and sex (Figure 4.4 - see overleaf). While most workers in each age group were employees, self-employment was more common among older workers than among the younger age groups. In spring 2004, 19 per cent of people aged 50 and over were self-employed compared with 14 per cent of people aged 25 to 49. Older men were more likely than older women to be self-employed: 26 per cent of men aged 50 and over compared with 11 per cent of women. Gender differences in self-employment become more marked after SPA – 46 per cent of men aged 65 and over were self-employed compared with 13 per cent of women aged 60–64 in 2004.

Self-employed men in their 50s were much more likely to be working ten years later than those who were employees. The same research also suggests that workers over SPA were twice as likely to be employed in companies with one to ten staff, and far less likely to be employed in organisations with over 50 staff. People aged 60 and over were particularly likely to be employed on a temporary basis and were more likely to work in small firms with fewer than 50 employees.

Figure **4.4**

Type of employment: by age and sex, spring 2004[1,2]

United Kingdom

Percentages

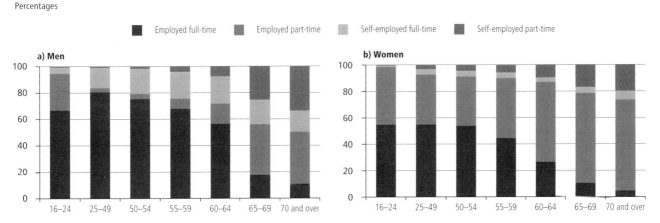

1 A small number of individuals who gave no answer to the full-time or part-time work question are excluded.
2 Survey respondent's views of whether they work full time or part time.

Source: Labour Force Survey, Office for National Statistics

For some older people, part-time work may act as a bridge between full-time work and retirement. In spring 2004 a slightly higher proportion of men aged 50 to SPA were working part time than ten years ago, 8 per cent compared with 5 per cent. However, part-time work remained relatively uncommon compared with full-time work for men below 65. For both men and women working after SPA working part time was more common than working full time. There was a greater tendency for women to work part time as they got older, with part-time employment (including part-time self-employment) accounting for 46 per cent of women working between 50 and SPA. The increase in the prevalence of part-time work occurred within industry sectors, though sector composition may have played a part in the overall figures.

The older people were when they left full-time employment, the less likely they were to make the transition to retirement through flexible working. The ability to negotiate flexible working arrangements depends on the skills and social networks people have built up during their working life.[1] The quality of flexible working can also depend on the type of employment. Self-employment is likely to offer similar job satisfaction and quality to full-time employment. Part-time employment can be less stable and offer fewer training opportunities. In spring 2004 older men with higher educational qualifications and people who had been employed in professional occupations were more likely to undertake self-employed work that was better paid.

Characteristics of older workers

Older workers have different characteristics than older people who are not participating in the labour market. They are more likely to have educational qualifications and be in a higher socio-economic group. They are also more likely to be part of a couple.

The higher the level of qualification an older person has attained the greater the probability of them being in employment. Overall 81 per cent of people aged between 50 and SPA with a degree were in employment, compared with 74 per cent of people with the equivalent of GCSEs and 52 per cent of people with no qualifications in 2004. The trend is similar for both men and women.

Figure 4.5 shows the employment rate pattern by highest qualification for men aged 25–49 and for those aged 50–59. The difference in employment rates by educational qualification is greater for the younger men, while for men in their 50s there was little difference for those with qualifications below degree level. The employment rates for those with no formal qualifications were substantially lower in both age groups.

Older people are less likely to have formal qualifications than younger groups – 23.5 per cent of those aged between 50 and 59 reported no formal qualifications compared with 11.2 per cent of those aged between 25 and 49 in 2004. Figure 4.6 identifies people with no qualifications, whether educational or work-related, by age group. The proportions rise quite steeply with age. This pattern is the result of successive birth cohorts gaining increasing numbers of qualifications and reflects the changes in participation at school and the subsequent increase in higher education across the generations for both men and women. Among older men with no qualifications there were particular increases in economic inactivity between 1993 and 2001.[6]

Figure **4.5**

Male employment rate: by highest qualification, spring 2004

United Kingdom
Percentages

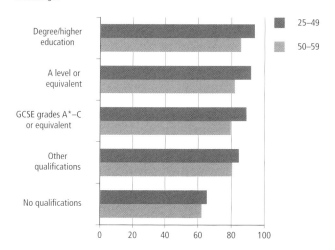

Source: Labour Force Survey, Office for National Statistics

Older people are also more likely to have skills related to declining industries.[7] Evidence suggests that older employees are less likely to do job-related training than younger employees.[8] In spring 2004 most employees aged between 50 and 69 had been encouraged by their employer to learn more job-related skills, but the proportion who did so was highest for those at the younger end of the group, those aged 50 to 54. Of all those aged between 50 and 69 and in work, 27 per cent said they had learnt to use new technology and received training in skills related to a specific job.[9]

Nearly three quarters (72.6 per cent) of people aged 50 and over in the higher managerial and professional group were employed compared with 58.6 per cent of people in the routine

Figure **4.6**

People with no formal qualifications: by age, 2003/04

United Kingdom
Percentages

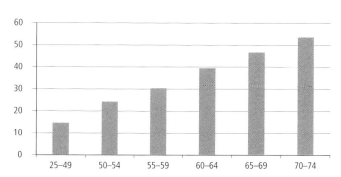

Source: Family Resources Survey, Department for Work and Pensions

occupations (Table 4.7). Older people in the 'small employers and own account workers' group had the highest overall employment rate (73.0 per cent). This group, which includes self-employed people and those working in small establishments that are not as restricted by employment practices, was also most likely to be working after age 65: 37.1 per cent compared with 10.5 per cent of people in the lower supervisory and technical group.

Table **4.7**

Employment rates: by socio-economic group[1], spring 2004

United Kingdom   Percentages

	50–54	55–59	60–64	65 and over	Total
Higher managerial & professional	93.6	80.8	59.9	29.3	72.6
Lower managerial & professional	92.0	80.0	52.5	22.6	70.2
Intermediate occupations	88.3	78.4	50.6	20.9	66.6
Small employers & own account workers	92.5	88.8	72.5	37.1	73.0
Lower supervisory & technical	86.5	78.0	49.3	10.5	60.2
Semi-routine occupations	82.1	77.0	52.1	20.7	60.8
Routine occupations	79.3	76.6	56.8	22.9	58.6

1 National Statistics Socio-economic Classification. Excludes those who have never worked and those unemployed for over eight years.

Source: Labour Force Survey, Office for National Statistics

Marital status, in particular the presence of a partner, is related to an older person's participation in the labour market. More than three quarters (77 per cent) of married and cohabiting couples where both partners are aged 50 and over reflected their partner's economic status: working people were more likely to have a working partner, while inactive people were more likely to have an inactive partner (Figure 4.8 – see overleaf). Over 29 per cent were working couples with both partners in employment and 48 per cent were workless couples where both partners were either unemployed or inactive. Where only one partner worked, this was more likely to be the man.

Older people who were married or cohabiting were also more likely to be in employment than people with no partner (never married, separated, divorced and widowed people). The employment rate in spring 2004 among people aged 50–54 who were married or cohabiting was 82 per cent compared with 69 per cent of people in the same age group with no partner. This trend was evident for all the older age groups.

Figure **4.8**

Labour market status of couples where both are aged 50 and over, spring 2004

United Kingdom

Percentages

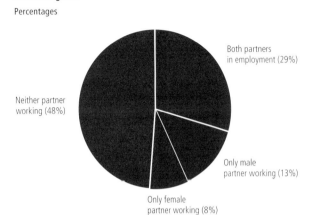

Source: Whiting (Reference 6) from Labour Force Survey, Office for National Statistics

Information from the Annual Survey of Hours and Earnings in the United Kingdom suggests that those people in work aged over 50 have lower average hourly earnings than those in their 40s, even when overtime earnings are excluded. Men aged 50 and over working full time in 2004 had median average gross earnings of £10.95 per hour, whereas those in their 40s earned £12.77 per hour. The observed relationship between wealth and the timing of retirement will affect this comparison, so it cannot be simply interpreted as a causal relationship between age and earnings for a given individual.[10]

Regional employment

There are substantial regional variations in the employment rate of older people, and the gap between older and younger people's employment rates. In the South East region of England the employment rate among people aged between 50 and SPA was 78 per cent in spring 2004, 13 percentage points lower than the rate for those aged between 25 and 49. This contrasts with the North East region, where the 50 to SPA employment rate was 61 per cent, 23 percentage points lower than for the 25 to 49 group.

In recent years there has been an increase in the proportions of people aged between 50 and SPA in employment across the United Kingdom. Between 1992 and 2004 the largest increases were in places where employment had previously been particularly low, such as the North East of England (Figure 4.9). There was also substantial variation within regions at local authority district level. In some local authority districts/unitary authorities the proportions of the 50 to SPA group claiming key out of work benefits fell by more than 10 percentage points between August 1995 and August 2003.

Figure **4.9**

Employment rate of people aged 50 to state pension age: by region

United Kingdom

Percentages

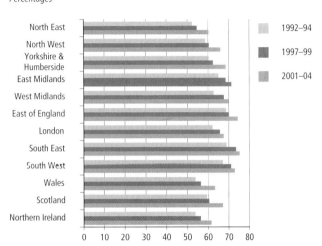

Source: Labour Force Survey, Office for National Statistics

Age, health and working

The proportion of the adult population with a long-standing illness is higher among people aged over 50 than for the adult population as a whole (see also Chapter 5: Health and well being). High proportions of people aged 50 to SPA claim benefits associated with sickness and disability, primarily Incapacity Benefit. About 1.2 million Incapacity Benefit claimants in the United Kingdom, almost half the total, were aged between 50 and SPA in February 2005.

Recent research suggests that 38 per cent of Incapacity Benefit recipients aged 50 to SPA were not seeking work but would like to work at some point in the future, but only 13 per cent of Incapacity Benefit recipients in this age group expected to work again. However, 63 per cent of people aged 50 to SPA on Incapacity Benefit who were not currently seeking work said that they might consider doing so if their health improved. Part-time paid work up to 30 hours per week was more likely to be considered than full-time work.[9]

Both age and health status have an impact on labour market participation. Overall employment levels for those with a long-standing illness and disability are substantially lower at each age than for those without (Figure 4.10). The employment rate was 57.8 per cent for people aged 50–54 with a disability or long-standing illness, compared with 87.2 per cent for the corresponding disability-free age group in 2003/04. The decline with age was similar irrespective of health status. The differences in the employment rates between people aged 25–49 and those aged 50–54 were generally small; the employment rate then fell for both those with a long-standing

Figure **4.10**

Employment rate: by health status and age, 2003/04

United Kingdom
Percentages

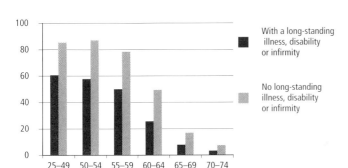

Source: Family Resources Survey, Department for Work and Pensions

illness, disability or infirmity and those without from age 55. Around a quarter (26 per cent) of those aged 60–64 with a long-standing illness, disability or infirmity were employed compared with half (50 per cent) of those without.[11]

Older people not in paid employment

About 2.7 million people aged between 50 and SPA in the United Kingdom were not in employment in spring 2004. The majority of those people not in work (28 per cent of the whole age group) were economically inactive rather than unemployed (see Figure 4.1) (see Glossary on page 38). Economic inactivity increases substantially with age from 18.9 per cent of people aged 50–54 to 93.9 per cent of people aged over 65 in spring 2004. Women are more likely to be inactive at an earlier age than men, partly because of the difference in SPA and also because women are more likely to take on caring responsibilities for elderly relatives and grandchildren.[1]

The most common occupations among people aged 50 and over who were inactive in 2004 were elementary occupations (17 per cent) and administrative and secretarial occupations (14 per cent). Inactive older people were least likely to have been previously employed in sales and customer service (7 per cent), personal service occupations (7 per cent) and associate professional and technical occupations (9 per cent).

The number of people aged 50 and over who were economically inactive increased by around 413,000 between spring 1994 and spring 2004, with a particular increase in the number of inactive men. However, the proportion who were

Figure **4.11**

Inactivity rates: by age, spring 1994 to spring 2004

United Kingdom
Percentages

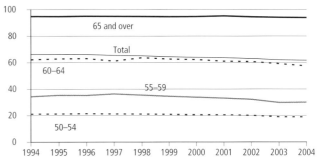

Source: Labour Force Survey, Office Naitonal Statistics

inactive fell over the same period by 4 percentage points to 61.7 per cent in spring 2004 because there was a proportionately larger increase in the total population of people aged 50 and over (Figure 4.11). For all men, the rate of inactivity decreased by nearly 3 percentage points over the decade, but there was an increase of almost 1 percentage point in the inactivity rate of men aged 50–54. The rate of inactivity for older women fell by nearly 6 percentage points to 68.5 per cent. Older people continued to be the largest inactive group, compared with other age groups.[1]

Once people aged 50 or over become economically inactive, they are likely to remain so for some time. Even if those aged over SPA are excluded, an estimated 94 per cent of individuals aged over 50 in Great Britain who were economically inactive 12 months ago were also inactive a year later. Older unemployed people are more likely to be long-term unemployed than their younger counterparts – 31 per cent of the unemployed aged 50 and over had been unemployed for more than a year compared with 25 per cent unemployed people aged between 25 and 49 in spring 2004.

Sickness, injury and disability was the reason given for not seeking work by more than half (58 per cent) of men out of work aged 50–54 in spring 2004; among men aged 65–69 the majority (83 per cent) classified themselves as retired (Figure 4.12 - see overleaf). Far higher proportions of older people who worked as process, plant and machine operatives (30 per cent) and in skilled trade occupations (29 per cent) were inactive for health reasons than those who worked in managerial and senior occupations, and professional occupations (both 15 per cent).

Figure **4.12**

Main reasons for being out of work: by age and sex, spring 2004

United Kingdom

Percentages

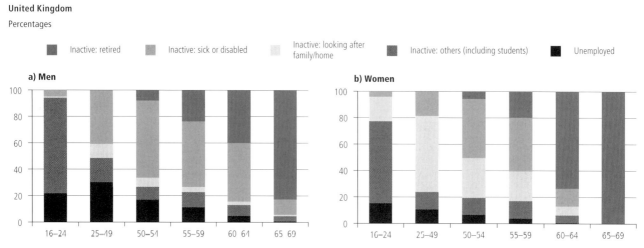

Source: Labour Force Survey, Office for National Statistics

Since 1994 there has been an overall decrease in the proportion of long-term sick and disabled men aged 50 to SPA, from 57 per cent to 53 per cent in 2004. This has been accompanied by a rise of nearly 8 percentage points in the proportion of retirees, to 31 per cent.

Among women there were similar patterns in the reasons for not seeking work. However a substantial proportion of older women under State Pension Age were not seeking work because they were looking after family or home: 30 per cent of those aged 50–54 and 22 per cent of those aged 55–59 (Figure 4.12). These reasons included providing care to sick and disabled people and childcare – as more parents are working, older people are increasingly caring for grandchildren.[1] The largest inactive group among women in their 50s in 1994 were those looking after the family/home (37 per cent), which included providing care. Since 1996 this has been overtaken by those classified as long-term sick and disabled, accounting for 42 per cent of women aged 50–59 in 2004.

The 2001 Census showed that more than one in five people aged 50 and over were providing care – the highest proportion for any age group.[1] Women were more likely than men to be carers in all age groups up to the age of 64. After age 65 there was a reversal, with men more likely to be carers than women. People aged over 49 accounted for about 178,000 (38 per cent) of Carer's Allowance claimants in February 2005. For some people the onset of caring obligations may affect their employment. In a study of people aged between 50 and 69 in 2003, almost one in ten people had seen their work pattern or employment opportunities affected by past or present caring responsibilities for someone sick, disabled or elderly.[9]

There is a distinction between those who are inactive voluntarily and those who have moved into inactivity involuntarily, perhaps through ill health or redundancy. A report by the Policy Innovation Unit in 2000 showed that about half of people aged between 50 and SPA who were not working received most of their income in state benefits and that an early exit from the labour market contributed substantially to poverty.[12]

Between 2002 and 2004, 16 per cent of process, plant and machine operatives were inactive because of redundancy compared with 4.6 per cent of people working in personal service occupations.[1] Research by the Social Exclusion Unit in 2004 showed that many older workers who lost their jobs following their employer closing down remained unemployed and became inactive, even when different job opportunities arose, because they did not have the relevant skills or had lost their confidence and self esteem.[13]

According to the first wave report of the English Longitudinal Study of Ageing (ELSA) there is a link between wealth and inactivity of older people. 'Early retirement' was clearly associated with high wealth levels.[10] Almost a quarter (24 per cent) of men in the richest wealth quintile described themselves as retired or semi-retired – around twice the proportion of all men aged 50 and over. The equivalent proportion for men in the poorest wealth quintile was 4 per cent.

The first wave of ELSA also revealed that the lowest two wealth groups are the likeliest to be inactive but not retired (Figure 4.13). In contrast the highest two wealth groups are the most likely to be inactive and retired. Those in the middle of the wealth distribution are the least likely to be inactive and

Figure **4.13**

Economic inactivity: by wealth quintile[1], age and sex, 2002

England

Percentages

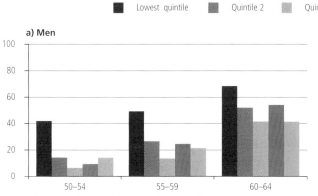
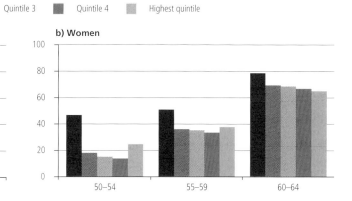

1 *Wealth quintiles are defined within each five-year age group.*

Source: English Longitudinal Study of Ageing, University College London

most likely to be in paid employment (see Chapter 7: Income, wealth and expenditure). Only 6 per cent of men in their early 50s were economically inactive compared with 16 per cent in the highest quintile and 44 per cent in the poorest quintile. By later ages the relationship between retirement or inactivity and wealth flattens out. The patterns are broadly similar for women at both the younger and older ages.

People in professional and managerial jobs were more likely than those in lower-skilled groups to have taken early retirement: 27 per cent and 24 per cent respectively. In contrast 6 per cent of people employed in elementary occupations and 7 per cent of those in sales and customer service occupations had done so during 2002–04.[1] Men in professional and senior roles were particularly likely to take early retirement (around 30 per cent), compared with women (17 per cent) in both categories.

The decision to retire is a complex one. It does not always consist of a straightforward move from work into inactivity, and does not necessarily coincide with State Pension Age. The 2003 *Report on the Factors Affecting the Labour Market Participation of Older Workers* [9] used a survey of people aged between 50 and 69 in Great Britain to look in detail at the retirement decision. Retirement status was defined by the respondent. Its findings included the following:

- Well over half (59 per cent) of fully retired men aged between 65 and 69 had retired before SPA and over a third (35 per cent) at SPA. For fully-retired women in the same age group just under a third (31 per cent) retired before SPA and 38 per cent at SPA. People with private pensions and those with health problems were among the groups most likely to retire before SPA.

- Half of those who were retired had wanted to retire. However, 39 per cent reported that they were forced into retirement. This was more common for those who retired before SPA due to ill health or redundancy; men (47 per cent) were more likely to have been forced to retire than women (33 per cent).

- People who were forced to retire before SPA were likely to find their post-retirement situation unsatisfying.

- There appeared to be a link between paying a mortgage and being in the labour market. Of people aged between 60 and 64 who were working and who didn't define themselves as retired in the survey, some 30 per cent were buying a property with a mortgage compared with only 15 per cent of fully retired people in the same age group. Previous analyses of factors linked to working past SPA also identify a link between having an outstanding mortgage and being in employment.[5]

- For people living with a partner, 64 per cent of those who had retired voluntarily and were fully retired, considered that the retirement decision had been jointly made with their partner.

Glossary

Economic activity

The number of people who are employed or unemployed as a percentage of the total population aged 16 and over. The economic activity rate is the percentage of the population, such as in a given age group, which is economically active.

Employment

The International Labour Organisation's definition of the employment rate is the percentage of people in a given age group who are in one or more hours of paid employment a week. The employment rate can be presented for any population group and is the proportion of that group who are in employment.

Unemployment

The measure based on International Labour Organisation guidelines and used in the Labour Force Survey counts as unemployed: people who are without a job, are available to start work in the next two weeks, who have been seeking a job in the last four weeks or are out of work and waiting to start a job already obtained in the next two weeks. The unemployment rate is the percentage of economically active people who are unemployed.

Economic inactivity

Economically inactive people are neither in employment nor unemployed, and are not actively seeking work, for example, people who have retired or are long-term sick. The Labour Force Survey categorises all economically inactive people who are more than five years above the State Pension Age as retired. The economic inactivity rate for an age group is the number of people who are inactive as a percentage of the total population of that age.

References

1 Whiting E (2005). The labour market participation of older people. *Labour Market Trends*, July 2005: 285–296.

2 Census information quoted in the *Employment Gazette* April 1995.

3 British Household Panel Survey, Institute for Social and Economic Research, in: Women and Men in the UK, *Facts and Figures 2000*. Cabinet Office.

4 *Welfare to work: tackling the barriers to the employment of older people*. National Audit Office. London: The Stationery Office. September 2004.

5 Smeaton D & McKay S (20 03). *Working after State Pension Age: a quantitative analysis* DWP Research Report **182**.

6 Barham C (2002). Patterns of economic inactivity among older men. *Labour Market Trends*. June 2002. (The result refers to the period autumn 1993 to autumn 2001.)

7 Campbell N (1999). *The decline of employment among older people in Britain*. Centre for Analysis of Social Exclusion.

8 *Partial Regulatory Impact Assessment for Age Discrimination Legislation*. Department of Trade and Industry. 2003.

9 *Factors affecting the labour market participation of older workers*. DWP Research Report **200**. 2003.

10 Banks J & Casanova M (2003). Work and retirement. In (eds) M Marmot, J Banks, R Blundell, C Lessof, J Nazroo. *Health, wealth and lifestyles of the older population in England: the 2002 English Longitudinal Study of Ageing*. Institute for Fiscal Studies. London.

11 Berthoud R (2003). *Multiple disadvantage in employment: a quantitative analysis*, Joseph Rowntree Foundation.

12 Policy Innovation Unit. (2000) *Winning the Generation Game*. Improving opportunities for people aged 50–65 in work and community activity. Cabinet Office. www.strategy/gov.uk/work_areas/active_ageing/index.asp

13 Social Exclusion Unit (2004) *Jobs and enterprise in deprived areas*. Office for the Deputy Prime Minister.

Further reading

Winning the Generation Game. Cabinet Office http://www.strategy/gov.uk/work_areas/active_ageing/index.asp

Older workers statistical information booklet. Biannual DWP publication. http://www.agepositive.gov.uk

Health and well being

Maria Evandrou
Centre for Research on Ageing, University
of Southampton

Key findings

- Women can expect to live longer than men, with life expectancy at birth in the UK in 2002 being 75.9 years for men and 80.5 years for women. However, women are also more likely to have more years in poor health; the expected years lived in poor health from age 65 onwards was 4.5 years for men and 5.8 years for women

- In 2003, just over a quarter of men aged 50–59 were current smokers compared with 23 per cent of women. The likelihood of smoking falls with age, reflecting both a 'healthy survivor' effect as well as patterns of smoking cessation. Over half of all smokers aged 50 and over reported wanting to give up smoking altogether

- Older people were more likely to drink alcohol frequently than younger people, and men were more likely than women. However, older people were less likely to have exceeded the recommended number of daily units in the last week compared to younger age groups

- Inequalities in health persist into later life. In the 2001 Census, 30 per cent of those aged 50 and over living in council rented accommodation reported a limiting long-term illness (LLTI) and 'not good' health over the last year, compared with 22 per cent of those residing in privately rented or rent free accommodation and just 14 per cent of owner occupiers

- Health varies by ethnicity: 27 per cent of all older people aged 50–64 reported a LLTI. However, this rose to 54 per cent among older people in the Bangladeshi group and 49 per cent among the Pakistanis, compared with just 20 per cent of Chinese origin

Chapter 5

Introduction

Health is an important dimension of quality of life among people of all ages[1] and takes on a particular resonance in later life[2]. Health and well being are complex notions, and the meaning attributed to questions concerning them is subjective. What constitutes good health varies according to people's experiences, expectations and social context.[3] Given this, there are a variety of approaches to measuring health and well being.[4] This chapter looks at trends in mortality and causes of death in later life, as well as patterns of self-reported health status, mental health, quality of life, daily living, health risk behaviour and health inequalities in later life.

Life expectancy

The expectation of life at a given age is defined as the average number of years that a person could be expected to live, if their risk of dying at each age were the same as that experienced in that calendar year. Thus it is a hypothetical measure, showing the average number of years a person would live if they lived their entire life under the conditions prevailing in that particular year.

Disability-Free Life Expectancy (DFLE) is calculated using data concerning older people's ability to perform five activities of daily living (ADL) based on the General Household Survey.

DFLE/Total life expectancy gives the proportion of remaining life at a given age that will be free from disability.

Mortality

The rise in life expectancy at birth has been one of the most significant achievements of the 20th century. In 1901 a man could expect to live, on average, for 45 years and a woman 49 years (Figure 5.1). By 2001 these figures had risen to 76 and 81

Figure 5.1

Trends in life expectancy[1] at birth, 1901 to 2041[2]

United Kingdom

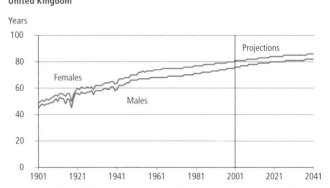

1 Expectation of life. The average number of years a new-born baby would survive if he or she experienced age-specific mortality rates for that time period throughout his or her life.
2 Data for 2001 onwards are from the 2003-based projections.

Source: Government Actuary's Department

years respectively. Much of the progress in the first part of the 20th century was due to improvements in infant and child mortality.

However, since the 1950s there have been significant declines in adult mortality, both in mid-life and more recently old age. Not only has there been an improvement in average survivorship at birth, but there has also been a marked rise in expectation of life at older ages. In 1981 a man aged 60 might have been expected to live a further 16.3 years if contemporary mortality rates continued to prevail (Table 5.2). By 2001 this had risen by 3.5 years to 19.8 years. Similar improvements occurred for older women, from 20.8 years in 1981 to 23.2 years in 2001.

It is not just years of life that are important, but also whether these years are lived in a disability-free state. Both total life expectancy (TLE) and disability-free life expectancy (DFLE) increased between 1980 and 1998 for all age groups of older men and women (Table 5.3).[5] For example, in 1980 a man

Table 5.2

Life expectancy at birth and selected ages: by sex, 1981 to 2001

United Kingdom

Years

	Men					Women				
	At birth	50	60	70	80	At birth	50	60	70	80
1981	70.8	24.1	16.3	10.1	5.8	76.8	29.2	20.8	13.3	7.5
1986	71.9	24.9	16.8	10.5	6.0	77.7	29.8	21.2	13.8	7.8
1991	73.2	26.0	17.7	11.1	6.4	78.7	30.6	21.9	14.3	8.2
1996	74.2	26.9	18.5	11.6	6.6	79.4	31.2	22.3	14.5	8.3
2001	75.7	28.3	19.8	12.5	7.1	80.4	32.1	23.2	15.1	8.7

Source: Government Actuary's Department

Table **5.3**.

Trends in life expectancy and disability free life expectancy, 1980 and 1998

Great Britain   Years/Percentages

	1980			1998		
	TLE[1]	DFLE[2]	DFLE/ TLE[3]	TLE[1]	DFLE[2]	DFLE/ TLE[3]
	(yrs)	(yrs)	(%)	(yrs)	(yrs)	(%)
Men						
65–69	12.9	11.6	*90*	15.4	14.2	*92*
70–74	10.0	8.6	*87*	12.1	10.9	*91*
75–79	7.6	6.2	*82*	9.3	8.1	*87*
80–84	5.8	4.1	*72*	7.0	5.6	*83*
85 and over	4.3	2.7	*61*	5.3	4.2	*79*
Women						
65–69	16.9	14.4	*85*	18.8	16.1	*86*
70–74	13.3	10.8	*81*	15.0	12.4	*82*
75–79	10.1	7.7	*76*	11.7	9.1	*78*
80–84	7.4	5.0	*67*	8.8	6.4	*73*
85 and over	5.3	2.7	*52*	6.6	4.3	*65*

1 TLE - total life expectancy.
2 DFLE - disability free life expectancy, based on five activities of daily living using the General Household Survey.
3 DFLE/TLE - gives the proportion of remaining life at a given age that will be free from disability.

Source: Bebbington, with Comas-Herrera (2000) (Reference 5)

aged 85 and over could have expected to live for an additional 4.3 years, of which 2.7 years would have been disability free. By 1998 these figures had risen to 5.3 years and 4.2 years respectively. Moreover, the rate of progress in DFLE has been greater than that of TLE, with the result that the proportion of remaining life that will be lived disability free (that is, DFLE/TLE) has risen. In 1980, for a man aged 85 and over, 61 per cent of remaining life could have been expected to be disability free. By 1998, this had risen to 79 per cent.

It is important to note that other calculations using different definitions have shown reverse trends. Estimates of healthy life expectancy based on self-reported health status over the last year from the General Household Survey show that in 1981 the expected years lived in poor health from age 65 onwards for men was 3.1 years, and for women was 5.0 years. By 2001, this had increased to 4.3 years and 5.8 years respectively.[6]

Currently, the main causes of death at ages over 50 are diseases of the circulatory system (including cardio-vascular disease and heart attacks), neoplasms (cancers), diseases of the respiratory system and those of the digestive system (Table 5.4). Death rates increase sharply with age and vary by sex. Neoplasms are the most important cause of death for women under 75 and men under 69, after which circulatory diseases are the main cause.

Table **5.4**

Death rates from selected underlying causes among persons aged 50 and over: by age and sex, 2003

England and Wales   Rates per 100,000 population

ICD–10 code	Underlying cause		Age						
			50–64	65–69	70–74	75–79	80–84	85 and over	All 50 and over
A00–R99, V01–Y89	**All causes, all ages**	M	**783**	**2,005**	**3,381**	**5,814**	**9,447**	**19,044**	**2,863**
		F	**491**	**1,234**	**2,142**	**3,858**	**6,646**	**16,576**	**2,850**
C00–D48	II Neoplasms	M	300	794	1,215	1,810	2,415	3,394	846
		F	256	543	797	1,105	1,393	1,837	658
I00–I99	IX Diseases of the circulatory system	M	275	757	1,346	2,401	4,062	7,813	1,147
		F	101	358	731	1,509	2,905	7,096	1,113
J00–J99	X Diseases of the respiratory system	M	57	195	397	825	1,494	3,882	404
		F	41	140	279	551	953	2,922	427
K00–K93	XI Diseases of the digestive system	M	59	91	123	196	315	648	119
		F	33	63	97	195	310	659	131
V01–Y89	XX External causes of morbidity and mortality	M	36	36	45	75	137	330	57
		F	15	19	26	58	107	328	52

Source: Derived by author from Tables 1 & 2 Mortality Statistics by Cause Series DH2 No 30, Office for National Statistics (2004)

Table **5.5**

General health status over the last year among people aged 50 and over: by age and sex, 2001

England and Wales

Percentages

	50–54	55–59	60–64	65–74	75–84	85 and over	All aged 50 and over
Men							
Good health	63	57	49	42	32	26	48
Fairly good health	25	28	31	39	43	42	33
Not good health	12	16	20	19	25	32	18
Women							
Good health	58	53	49	39	29	22	43
Fairly good health	29	31	36	42	43	42	37
Not good health	13	16	16	19	28	36	20

Source: Census 2001, Office for National Statistics

Self-reported health status and mental health

The 2001 Census included questions on both general health status over the last twelve months, and whether people reported a long-term illness, health problem or disability which limits their daily activities or work (including problems of old age). The majority of older people in England and Wales reported being in 'good' or 'fairly good' health over the last year with around a fifth of older people reporting 'not good' health (Table 5.5).

The proportion reporting 'not good' health increased with age from 12–13 per cent for men and women aged 50–54 to over 30 per cent for those aged 85 and over (Figure 5.6). While the gap between the sexes was generally small, it was particularly pronounced at ages 60–64 when 20 per cent of men reported 'not good health', compared with 16 per cent of women. In contrast, at ages 75 and over, women were more likely to report poor health than men: 28 per cent of women aged 75–84 were in 'not good health' compared with 25 per cent of men.

There was a similar picture with regard to limiting long-term illness (LLTI). Interestingly, men aged 60–74 were more likely to report a LLTI than women (Figure 5.7). This may reflect differences in health or sex-specific health expectations. The proportion reporting a LLTI rose with age. Among men aged 85 and over, 70 per cent reported having a LLTI compared with just 20 per cent of men aged 50–54.

Many older people still considered themselves to be in good health, even if they had a long-term illness that limited their daily activity. In 2001, of all men aged 65 and over reporting a LLTI, 12 per cent considered themselves in 'good health' over the previous year and 46 per cent reported being in 'fairly

Figure **5.6**

Older people reporting 'not good' health over the last 12 months: by age and sex, 2001

England and Wales

Percentages

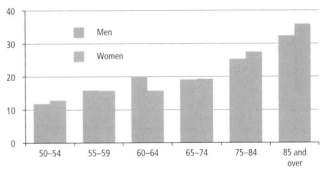

Source: Census 2001, Office for National Statistics

Figure **5.7**

Older people reporting a limiting long-term illness: by age and sex, 2001

England and Wales

Percentages

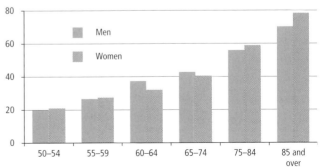

Source: Census 2001, Office for National Statistics

good health'. Similarly, for older women with a LLTI, 11 per cent reported being in 'good health' and 45 per cent in 'fairly good health'.[7]

It is not just physical health that is key to the quality of life of older people, but also mental health. The English Longitudinal Survey of Ageing (ELSA) included two measures of symptomatic mental ill health, as well as asking respondents if they had ever been diagnosed with any emotional, nervous or psychiatric problems.[8] The 12-item General Health Questionnaire (GHQ-12) is a widely used and validated measure of psychological well being, where respondents are grouped according to the number of symptoms reported. Having four or more symptoms is an established indicator of mental ill health.[9] ELSA also included a shortened version (8-item) of the Center for Epidemiologic Studies Depression Scale (CES-D), including questions on experiences of loneliness, depression, restless sleep, feeling unhappy etc over the last month.[10] Respondents were classified as being depressed if they reported 3 or more symptoms.

Older women were more likely to report symptomatic mental ill health than men (Table 5.8): 14 per cent of women reported 4 or more symptoms on the GHQ-12 and 28 per cent were classified as suffering from depression (CES-D, 3+ symptoms), compared with 12 per cent and 20 per cent, respectively, among older men. The proportion with poor mental health was highest among those older people aged 80 and over, and lowest among those in the middle age groups (60–64 and 65–69).

Interestingly, the proportion of older people with a diagnosed mental illness was markedly lower than the prevalence of symptomatic mental ill health (as measured by GHQ-12 and CES-D). Moreover, in contrast to the trend for symptomatic mental illness, the prevalence of diagnosed mental illness declined with age. This may reflect the fact that depression among older people often goes undiagnosed and therefore untreated.

ELSA also collected information on the quality of life of older people using the CASP-19 questionnaire, which includes questions on control, autonomy, self-realisation and pleasure.[11] According to this measure, older men and women enjoyed similar levels of well being, with 61 per cent of those aged 50 and over reporting above-average quality of life (Table 5.8). The rates varied with age, with those aged 80 and over reporting much lower rates of above-average quality of life than younger age groups: 39 per cent for men and 43 per cent for women aged 80 and over, compared with 64 per cent for both men and women aged 50–54.

Daily living

Questions concerning older people's ability to undertake 'activities of daily living' (ADLs, for example, bathing, continence, dressing, feeding) and 'instrumental activities of daily living' (IADLs, for example, managing finances, preparing meals or doing shopping) provide a good guide regarding their ability to live independently in the community. Overall, 21 per cent of women and 12 per cent of men aged 65 and over were

Table **5.8**

Mental health and well being among people aged 50 and over: by age and sex, 2002

England   Percentages

	50–54	55–59	60–64	65–69	70–74	75–79	80 and over	All aged 50 and over
Men								
GHQ12 score 4+[1]	14	14	10	10	10	12	16	12
CES-D 3+ symptoms[2]	19	20	20	19	17	23	26	20
Diagnosed mental illness	9	7	6	5	4	3	3	6
Above average quality of life	64	61	65	64	62	52	39	61
Women								
GHQ12 score 4+[1]	16	15	12	11	12	16	19	14
CES-D 3+ symptoms[2]	26	25	23	26	31	34	37	28
Diagnosed mental illness	13	13	9	7	6	5	5	9
Above average quality of life	64	64	68	65	59	56	43	61

1   General Health Questionnaire (GHQ-12) - a score of 4 or more symptoms is an indicator of mental ill health.
2   Centre for Epidemiologic Studies Depression Scale (CES-D) - a score of 3 or more is classified as depression.

Source: English Longitudinal Study of Ageing, University College London

unable to carry out at least one of the activities listed in Table 5.9. Activities of daily living likely to cause most difficulty among older people were going out of doors and walking down the road and managing up and down stairs. Around a third of women, and a quarter of men, aged 65 and over reported some difficulty getting around the house (Table 5.9). Sixteen per cent of the older women could only go out of doors and walk down the road with help.

Difficulties in performing ADLs increase with age (Figure 5.10). Three per cent of older people aged 65–69 could not manage steps or stairs unaided. This rose to 13 per cent among those aged 85 and over. The proportion of women unable to negotiate these activities was higher than among men across these age groups. For example, 27 per cent of women aged 85 and over could not manage stairs and steps on their own compared with 19 per cent of men in the same age group.[12]

Over time, the proportion of older people reporting difficulties with ADLs has been relatively stable. In 1980, 12 per cent of people aged 65 and over reported that they were unable to walk out of doors on their own, compared with 14 per cent in 2001.

Research using the ONS Survey of Psychiatric Morbidity in 2000 found that among people aged 60–74, the likelihood of reporting difficulties with at least one ADL increased both with the level of long-term physical health problems and the level of mental disorders. At every level of physical ill health, people with mental disorders were more likely to have difficulty with ADLs than those without.[13]

Healthy ageing

Health in later life in part depends upon people's lifestyles. Two important health risk behaviours are smoking and drinking. Reducing smoking is one of the three key commitments of the NHS Cancer Plan[14] as smoking has been found to be the cause of a third of all cancers[15]. The prevalence of smoking among older people has shown little change over the period 1998 to 2003 (Table 5.11). In 2003, just over a quarter (26 per cent) of men aged 50–59 were current smokers compared with 23 per cent of women. The likelihood of smoking falls with age, reflecting both a 'healthy survivor' effect as well as patterns of smoking cessation.

Over half of all smokers aged 50 and over reported wanting to give up smoking altogether (Figure 5.12). Older smokers were the least likely to want to stop smoking: 48 per cent of those aged 65–74, compared with 62 per cent of those aged 60–64, and 65 per cent of those aged 50–59. Given that smoking prevalence is lower among older age groups, it is likely that those smokers who may have wished to give up smoking have already done so by the age of 75, or that they have died.

44

Table **5.9**

Ability to carry out various activities of daily living among persons aged 65 and over living in private households[1], 2001/02

Great Britain — Percentages

Task	Men	Women
Difficulty managing stairs		
On own, no difficulty	78	72
On own, with some difficulty	15	18
Only with help, or not at all	7	11
Difficulty going out of doors and walking down the road		
On own, no difficulty	79	75
On own, with some difficulty	12	9
Only with help, or not at all	9	16
Difficulty using the toilet		
On own, no difficulty	75	75
On own, with some difficulty	20	20
Only with help, or not at all	5	5
Difficulty getting around the house		
On own, no difficulty	70	65
On own, with some difficulty	25	32
Only with help, or not at all	5	3
Difficulty getting in and out of bed		
On own, no difficulty	70	68
On own, with some difficulty	21	26
Only with help, or not at all	9	6

1 Age standardised using the European standard population.

Source: Author's analysis using General Household Survey, Office for National Statistics

Figure **5.10**

Older people reporting difficulties in getting up and down stairs/steps: by age, 2001/02

Great Britain

Percentages

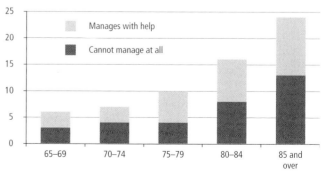

Source: General Household Survey, Office for National Statistics

Table **5.11**

Prevalence of cigarette smoking among persons aged 35 and over: by age and sex, 1998 to 2003

Great Britain

Percentages

	1998	2000	2001	2002	2003
Men					
35-49	33	31	31	29	32
50-59	28	27	26	27	26
60 and over	16	16	16	17	16
Women					
35-49	29	27	28	27	28
50-59	27	28	25	24	23
60 and over	16	15	17	14	14

Source: General Household Survey, Office for National Statistics

Older people were more likely to drink alcohol frequently than younger people, and men were more likely than women (Figure 5.13).[16] For example, 30 per cent of men aged 75 and over had drunk alcohol on five or more days in the previous week compared with just 14 per cent of men aged 16–24. However, older people were less likely to have exceeded the recommended number of daily units in the last week (Figure 5.14). Around a quarter of men aged 65–74 had exceeded the daily benchmark compared with nearly half of young men (aged 16–24). For women, just over one in twenty (65–74) exceeded the benchmark, while around four in ten young women (16–24) did so.

Participation in social activities is important for physical and mental well being. The proportion of older people who reported being a member of a sports club, gym or exercise

Figure **5.12**

Current smokers who would like to stop smoking altogether: by age and sex, 2003/04

Great Britain

Percentages

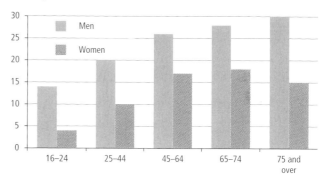

Source: General Household Survey, Office for National Statistics

Figure **5.13**

People who had drunk alcohol on five days or more in the week prior to interview: by age and sex, 2003/04

Great Britain

Percentages

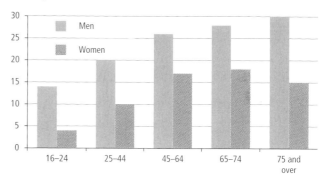

Source: General Household Survey, Office for National Statistics

Figure **5.14**

Older people exceeding daily benchmarks for drinking[1]: by sex and age, 2003/04

Great Britain

Percentages

a) Men

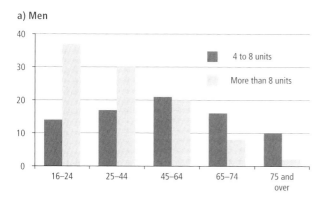

b) Women

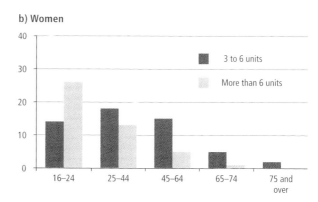

1 *Drank more than four units (men) or three units (women) on at least one day last week.*

Source: General Household Survey, Office for National Statistics

class varied by age and sex (Table 5.15). Membership was highest in the younger age groups (50–54 and 55–59). At ages below 70, more women were members of a sports club than men, but for ages 70–74 and 80 and over this differential was reversed. There was a relationship between sports club membership and general health status, with only 8 per cent of all men over 50 who reported being in 'fair/poor' health being a member compared with 18 per cent of those in 'good' health and 24 per cent of those in 'excellent/very good' health.[17] It is difficult to determine the direction of causation as poor health may act as a barrier to participation in physical activity, and equally regular exercise may contribute to good health.

Interestingly, the pattern of membership by age was reversed for membership of a church or religious organisation, with rates of membership being over twice as great in the age group 80 and over (36 per cent for women, 23 per cent for men) as in the age group 50–54 years (17 per cent and 11 per cent, respectively). A detailed discussion of patterns of leisure and social behaviour in later life is presented in Chapter 8.

In 2001 almost 2.8 million people aged 50 and over (16 per cent) living in private households in England and Wales provided unpaid care for family members, friends or neighbours. People in their 50s were the group most likely to be providing unpaid care. More than one in five (21 per cent) were doing so. The proportion declined with age. Even so, 5 per cent of those aged 85 and over were providing some form of unpaid care. Among 50 to 64 year olds a greater proportion of women than men provide unpaid care. However, for the older age groups men are more likely than women to be providing care. One in four carers over the age of 50 (24 per cent) spent 50 hours or more a week caring. This proportion rose to one in two carers aged 85 and over (50 per cent).[18] The provision and receipt of unpaid care in later life is discussed in more detail in Chapter 6.

Inequalities in health

Although life expectancy at older ages has improved across time, significant differences in life expectancy at age 65 by previous occupation remain: 17.5 years for men from Social Class I ('Professionals' such as doctors, chartered accountants), compared with 13.4 years for men from Social Class V ('Manual unskilled' such as labourers, cleaners and messengers). The figures for women are 20.8 and 16.3 years respectively.[19] Tackling health inequalities is a key priority and in July 2003 the Government published its strategy *Tackling Health Inequalities: A Programme for Action.*[20] Its main focus is on narrowing the health gap between disadvantaged groups, communities and the rest of the country, and on improving health overall. This section presents evidence on how the health of older people varies across different ethnic groups, housing tenure, social class and income.

Ethnicity

There is significant diversity in the prevalence of chronic ill health and disability in later life by ethnicity.[21] Using data from the 2001 Census, 27 per cent of all people aged 50–64 reported a LLTI. However this rose to 54 per cent among people of Bangladeshi origin and 49 per cent among those of Pakistani origin, compared with just 20 per cent of Chinese

Table 5.15

Physical and social activity among people aged 50 and over: by age and sex, 2002

England

Percentages

	50–54	55–59	60–64	65–69	70–74	75–79	80 and over	All aged 50 and over
Men								
Member of sports club, gym or exercise class	24	21	18	19	17	11	9	19
Church or other religious group	11	12	17	16	21	22	23	16
Women								
Member of sports club, gym or exercise class	26	23	22	23	13	12	5	19
Church or other religious group	17	19	28	27	27	34	36	25

Source: English Longitudinal Study of Ageing, University College London

origin. Health differentials between ethnic groups were less marked among individuals aged 65 and over. Nevertheless a significantly higher proportion of individuals from South Asian backgrounds reported a LLTI than their White counterparts (Figure 5.16).

Health also varies by sex within ethnic groups (Figure 5.17). Among all people aged 65 and over, a higher proportion of women than men reported a long-standing illness that limits their activity (53 per cent against 49 per cent). The differential between women and men was greater among older Indians, Pakistanis, Other Asians, Black Others and Black Africans. Among Bangladeshi elders, the differential was reversed with a higher proportion of men reporting a LLTI (65 per cent) than women (59 per cent).

Figure **5.16**

Reporting of a limiting long-term illness in older people: by age and ethnic group, 2001

England and Wales

Percentages

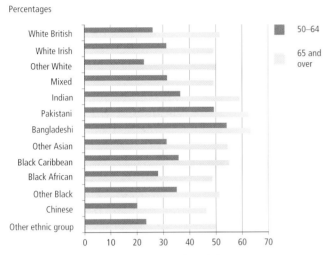

Source: Census 2001, Office for National Statistics

Housing tenure

Health differentials in later life are also found according to people's housing tenure. Among all people aged 50 and over, 17 per cent reported a LLTI and 'not good' health over the last year in the 2001 Census. This varied markedly across housing tenure, with 30 per cent of those aged 50 and over living in council rented accommodation reporting such ill health, compared with 22 per cent of those residing in privately rented or rent free accommodation and 14 per cent of owner occupiers. Health inequalities across housing tenures persisted throughout later life, although they narrowed with rising age (Figure 5.18). Those living in social housing reported the highest rates of ill health. The proportion for those aged 50–54 was 3.5 times greater for those renting from the council compared with owner occupiers, while for those aged 85 and over, it was a fifth greater.

Figure **5.17**

Limiting long-term illness in people aged 65 and over: by ethnic group and sex, 2001

England and Wales

Percentages

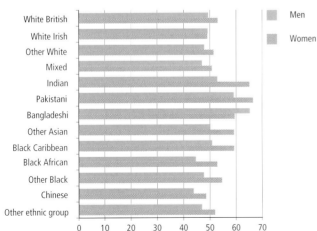

Source: Census 2001, Office for National Statistics

Figure **5.18**

People aged 50 and over reporting a limiting long-term illness and 'not good' health over the past year: by housing tenure, 2001

England and Wales

Percentages

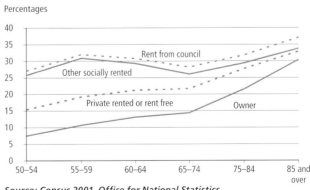

Source: Census 2001, Office for National Statistics

Socio-economic status

Inequalities in health in later life are also found by socio-economic classification (Figures 5.19 and 5.20). A greater proportion of individuals from semi-routine and routine occupations reported a long-standing illness that limited their activities (LLTI) than those who had worked in managerial and professional occupations (Figure 5.19). For example, among those aged 50–59, 20 per cent from semi-routine and routine occupations reported a LLTI compared with 13 per cent of those from managerial and professional occupations. Among

those aged 50–74, the gradient by occupation widened in the 60–64 age group, after which it flattened out. This may reflect the healthy survivor effect, as those in worst health die.

The highest proportions reporting a LLTI were found among those older people who have never worked or who are 'not classified for other reasons' (Figure 5.20). This reflects the fact that ability to work is affected by health status. An advantage of increased longevity is the option of life-long learning. Older people who were full-time students reported better health than other groups who were out of the labour market.

Figure **5.19**

People aged 50–74[1] reporting a limiting long-term illness: by NS-SEC[2] and age, 2001

England and Wales

Percentages

a) 50 to 59 years

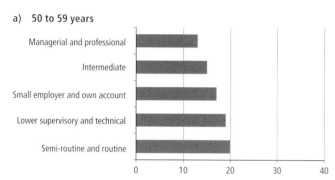

b) 60 to 64 years

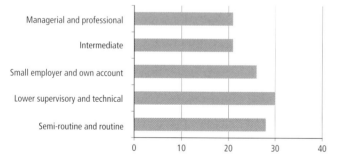

c) 65 to 74 years

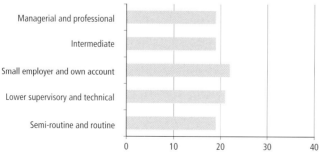

1 All older people living in private households.
2 National Statistics socio-economic classification.

Source: Census 2001, Office for National Statistics

Figure **5.20**

People aged 50–74[1] reporting a limiting long-term illness: by economic inactivity and age, 2001

England and Wales

Percentages

a) 50 to 59 years

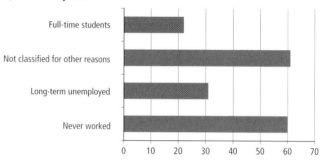

b) 60 to 64 years

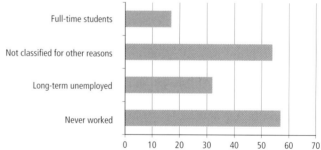

c) 65 to 74 years

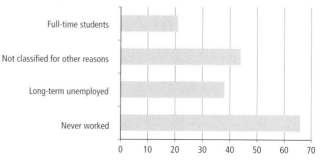

1 All older people living in private households.

Source: Census 2001, Office for National Statistics

However their prevalence of LLTI was similar to that found among those in lower supervisory and technical occupations.

Health differences by socio-economic classification are less marked among older women than men at ages 50–64. For example, among women aged 50–59 the difference in the prevalence of LLTI between those in managerial and professional occupations and those in semi-routine and routine occupations was 6 percentage points compared with a gap of 9 percentage points among men of the same age. After 65, health inequalities appear less pronounced, with a gap of around 1 percentage point for those aged 65–74 years.

There are also clear occupational class gradients in measures of symptomatic mental ill health. Men in managerial and professional occupations were least likely to score 4 or more on the GHQ12 (10 per cent) and men in routine or manual occupations were most likely (14 per cent). Similarly both men and women in managerial and professional households were less likely to be depressed than those in manual households (as measured by CES-D 3+).[22]

Income

Health inequalities are also found across income groups (Figure 5.21). The proportion of people aged 50 and over reporting a LLTI in the 2001 General Household Survey was 35 per cent. This varied from 45 per cent among those living in households in the bottom fifth of the income distribution to 19 per cent living in the top fifth. This gradient was steepest among those aged 50–59 and flattest among those aged 75 and over.

Figure 5.21

People aged 50 and over with a limiting long-term illness in the top and bottom quintiles of equivalent gross household income[1], 2001/02

Great Britain

Percentages

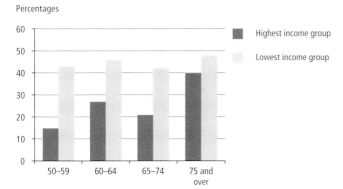

1 Lowest income quintile group: £164.20 or below weekly income. Highest quintile group: £681.31 and above weekly income.

Source: Author's analysis using General Household Survey, Office for National Statistics

Income comparisons

The income distribution was calculated using equivalised gross weekly household income. The equivalent scale used takes into account differences in the number of adults and children in the household.

Material deprivation has been found to be one of the main drivers of health differences in later life.[21] The Acheson Report, *Health Inequalities*,[23] and more recently the Government initiative *Tackling Health Inequalities*, recognise that policies to reduce social and economic inequalities should be a key part of any strategy to reduce inequalities in health. The income position of older people is discussed in Chapter 7.

References

1   Sen AK (1985) *Commodities and Capabilities*, Amsterdam: North Holland.

2   Walker A and Hagan Hennessy C (2004) *Growing Older: Quality of Life in Old Age*. London: McGraw-Hill.

3   Blaxter M (2004) *Health*. Bristol: Polity Press.

4   Bowling A (1997) *Measuring Health: A Review of Quality of Life Measurement Scales*. 2nd edition. Buckingham: Open University Press.

5   Bebbington A with Comas-Herrera A (2000) *Healthy Life Expectancy: Trends to 1998 and the implications for long term care costs*. PSSRU Discussion Paper no. **1695**. Kent, PSSRU, December 2000.

6   Office for National Statistics (2004) Focus on Health. http://www.statistics.gov.uk/focuson/health/

7   Office for National Statistics (2003) *Census 2001, National Report for England & Wales*, London: TSO. Table S016, pp.40–41.

8   Marmot M, Banks J, Blundell R, Lessof C & Nazroo J (eds) (2003) *Health, welfare and lifestyles of the older population in England: The 2002 English Longitudinal Study of Ageing*. London: IFS.

9   Goldberg D & Williams P (1988) *Users Guide to the General Health Questionnaire*, NFER-Nelson.

10 Shumaker S, Schron E & Ockene J (eds) (1990) *The Handbook of Health Behavior Change*. New York: Springer-Verlag.

11 Hyde M, Wiggins RD, Higgs P & Blane D (2003) A Measure of Quality of Life in Early Old Age: The theory, development and properties of a needs satisfaction model (CASP-19). *Age and Mental Health*, **7**:186–194.

12 Office for National Statistics (2003) *People aged 65 and over*:
    Results of a study carried out by the Department of Health as part
    of the 2001 General Household Survey. London: TSO.

13 Evans O, Singleton N, Meltzer H, Stewart R & Prince M (2003) *The
    Mental Health of Older People.* London: TSO.

14 Department of Health (2000) *The NHS Cancer Plan.* London: TSO.
    www.doh.gov.uk/cancer/cancerplan/htm

15 Health Education Authority (1998) *The UK Smoking Epidemic*:
    Deaths in 1995. London: HEA.

16 Office for National Statistics (2002) *Living in Britain*: *Results from
    the 2001 General Household Survey.* London: TSO.

17 Hyde M & Janevic M (2003). Social activity. In (eds) M Marmot, J
    Banks, R Blundell, C Lessof, J Nazroo. *Health, wealth and lifestyles
    of the older population in England: the 2002 English Longitudinal
    Study of Ageing.* Institute for Fiscal Studies. London. Table 5A.**10**,
    p.189.

18 Office for National Statistics (2004) Focus on Older People. http://
    www.statistics.gov.uk/focuson/olderpeople/

19 Donkin A, Goldblatt P & Lynch K (2002) Inequalities in life
    expectancy by social class, 1972–1999, *Health Statistics Quarterly*
    15:5–15. London: TSO.

20 Department of Health (2003) *Tackling Health Inequalities*: A
    Programme for Action. London: Department of Health
    Publications.

21 Evandrou M (2000) Ethnic inequalities in health in later life, *Health
    Statistics Quarterly*, **8**: 20–28.

22 McMunn A, Hyde M, Janevic M & Kumari M (2003). Health. In
    (eds) M Marmot, J Banks, R Blundell, C Lessof, J Nazroo. *Health,
    wealth and lifestyles of the older population in England: the 200
    English Longitudinal Study of Ageing.* Institute for Fiscal Studies.
    London. Table 6A.**17**, p.242.

23 Acheson D (1998) *Independent Inquiry into Inequalities in Health.*
    London: TSO.

Health and social care

Maria Evandrou
Centre for Research on Ageing, University of Southampton

Chapter 6

Key findings

- In 2002/03 a fifth of people aged 50 and over had consulted a GP and one in ten had seen a practice nurse in the last 2 weeks. One in five older people had attended an outpatient or casualty department in the previous year and one in ten had a hospital inpatient stay

- The majority of older people continue to live in the community well into later life; three quarters of people aged 90 and over were living in private households in 2001

- An estimated 3.4 million contact hours were provided by councils in 2004 to around 355,600 households, compared with 2.2 million hours in 1994. However, the number of households receiving council funded home care services has fallen consistently since 1994, suggesting that councils are providing more intensive services to a smaller number of households

- Family members supply the majority of social care provided in the community. In 2001 over three-quarters of all older people who reported suffering from mobility problems were helped by their spouse or other household members

- As well as receiving informal care, older people are also major providers of care. In 2001, 1.2 million men and 1.6 million women aged 50 and over in England and Wales were providing unpaid care to family members, neighbours or relatives – representing 16 per cent of men and 17 per cent of women aged 50 and over

Introduction

Older people are key users of health and social care services. In 2002/03 people aged 65 and over, comprising 16 per cent of the population, accounted for 47 per cent of total spending on hospital and community health services in England (Figure 6.1).[1] In contrast, children aged 5–15 accounted for just 4 per cent of health spending but made up 14 per cent of the population. High health care costs are associated with birth, but expenditure per head then decreases sharply and remains relatively low through young and middle age. After age 65, the level of spending per person rises sharply with age, reflecting the greater use of health services by older people (Figure 6.2). This chapter explores patterns of use of health and social care services by people aged 50 and over, examining how utilisation varies with age, gender and ill health.

Figure **6.1**

Gross current expenditure on hospital and community health services: by age, 2002/03

England

Percentages

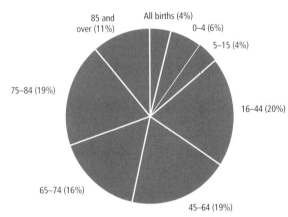

Source: Department of Health

Figure **6.2**

Hospital and community health service gross current expenditure per head: by age, 2002/03

England

£ per head

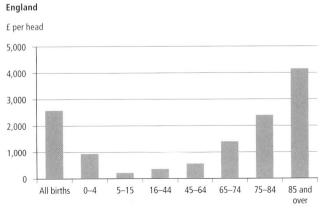

Source: Department of Health

Health service use

Primary health care

The General Household Survey (GHS) collects information on the use of health services among older people. In 2002/03 just over a fifth (21 per cent) of people aged 50 and over had consulted a General Practitioner (GP) in the two weeks before interview, and one in ten had seen a practice nurse in the same period. People visit Primary Care Trusts for a variety of reasons, including health checks, information, vaccinations, prescriptions, and ill health. The proportion of older people reporting a long-standing illness that limits their activity rises with age (see Chapter 5: Health), therefore it is not surprising that utilisation of primary health care services varied by age, with individuals in older age groups being more likely to see a GP or practice nurse than younger age groups (Table 6.3).

Taking physical health into account, within each age group older people with a limiting long-term illness (LLTI) were more

Table **6.3**

People aged 50 and over who report using health services: by age and sex, 2002/03[1]

Great Britain

Percentages

	50–64	65–74	75 and over
GP in the last 2 weeks			
Men	18	23	23
Women	20	23	28
All	19	23	26
Practice nurse in the last 2 weeks			
Men	6	13	11
Women	8	12	12
All	7	12	12
Outpatient in the last 3 months			
Men	16	24	26
Women	16	20	25
All	16	22	25
Day-patient in last 12 months			
Men	8	11	12
Women	8	10	10
All	8	10	11
Inpatient in the last 12 months			
Men	8	15	18
Women	8	8	16
All	8	11	17

1 Using weighted data.

Source: Author's analysis using General Household Survey, Office for National Statistics

likely to use health services than those without. For example, among those aged 50–64, 32 per cent of those with a LLTI reported consulting a GP in the last two weeks and 12 per cent saw a practice nurse, compared with 13 and 5 per cent respectively among those with no LLTI of the same age (Table 6.4). Among those older people without a LLTI, GP utilisation rates increased with age, which may reflect increased monitoring of those aged 75 and over via GP health checks. There is no clear gradient in utilisation by age among those older people with a LLTI.

The likelihood of older people consulting a GP is also associated with mental ill health. Research using the ONS Psychiatric Morbidity Survey 2000 examining community based and hospital service use by mental disorder found that a higher proportion of older people with mental health problems, defined as having a CIS-R score of 12 or more, had consulted a GP in the last year compared with those with lower CIS-R scores (Table 6.5).[2] Interestingly, this was the case for GP consultations concerning physical health problems as well as those relating to mental health problems. For example, among

Table 6.4

Persons aged 50 and over using health care services: by whether they reported a limiting long-term illness (LLTI), 2002/03[1]

Great Britain   Percentages

	50–64		65–74		75 and over	
	With LLTI	Without LLTI	With LLTI	Without LLTI	With LLTI	Without LLTI
GP/doctor (last 2 weeks)	32	13	32	16	31	21
Practice nurse (last 2 weeks)	12	5	15	10	13	10
Hospital outpatient (last 3 months)	28	11	32	15	33	16
Hospital day patient (last year)	14	6	15	7	13	8
Hospital inpatient (last year)	17	5	19	6	23	10

1 Using weighted data.

Source: Author's analysis using General Household Survey, Office for National Statistics

Table 6.5

Use of health care services by people aged 60–74: by CIS-R score[1] and age, 2000

Great Britain   Percentages

	60–64		65–69		70–74	
	Score less than 12	Score 12 and over	Score less than 12	Score 12 and over	Score less than 12	Score 12 and over
Any GP visit in last year	68	91	73	94	73	93
Visited GP with physical complaint	66	88	72	92	72	89
Visited GP with mental complaint	6	33	4	20	6	36
Had any outpatient visit in last year	19	49	24	45	27	29
Outpatient visit with physical complaint	19	49	24	44	27	29
Outpatient visit with mental complaint	0	0	0	2	1	..
Had any inpatient stay in last year	3	5	4	15	4	7
Inpatient stay with physical complaint	3	5	4	15	4	5
Inpatient stay with mental complaint	..	..	..	..	..	2
Received any community care in last year	4	10	6	19	6	23

1 A CIS-R score of 12 or above indicates a diagnosis of a neurotic disorder. Data available for individuals up to age 74.

Source: Survey of Psychiatric Morbidity, Office for National Statistics

people aged 70–74, 89 per cent of those with a CIS-R score of 12 or more had consulted a GP for a physical health problem compared with 72 per cent of those with a lower CIS-R score.

Mental disorder was assessed using the revised version of the Clinical Interview Schedule (CIS-R) which is based upon 14 individual symptoms including sleep problems, irritability, depression, phobias, obsessions, fatigue, anxiety, panic, concentration and forgetfulness.[3] Scores range between 0 and 57, and a score of 12 and above is taken to represent a diagnosis of a neurotic disorder.

Of all people aged 50 and over who consulted a GP in the previous two weeks, 81 per cent visited their GP at the surgery or health centre, 7 per cent saw the doctor at home and 7 per cent consulted by phone. The site of the consultation varies with age, with home visits being much more likely among those aged 75 and over compared with younger age groups (Table 6.6). Women are more likely than men to receive a home visit, and this differential is marked among those aged 75 and over, with 16 per cent of women doing so compared with 13 per cent of men of the same age. Of those older

Table **6.6**

NHS GP consultations by site and whether prescription obtained: by age and sex, 2002/03[1]

Great Britain			Percentages
	50–64	65–74	75 and over
Men			
Doctor's surgery	76	78	69
Home	2	4	13
Telephone	6	9	7
Health centre	6	7	5
Elsewhere	10	2	6
Women			
Doctor's surgery	79	75	63
Home	3	7	16
Telephone	7	5	11
Health centre	7	7	7
Elsewhere	5	7	4
Obtained prescription			
Men	63	72	66
Women	66	72	68
All	65	72	67

1 Using weighted data.

Source: Author's analysis using General Household Survey, Office for National Statistics

people consulting a GP, 67 per cent obtained a prescription, with older age groups being slightly more likely to do so than the 50–64 age group, although the gradient with age is not uniform (Table 6.6). NHS prescriptions are free for those 60 and over.

Over the last 30 years, there has been a slight rise in the proportions of older people aged 45–64 who consulted an NHS GP in the previous two weeks (Figure 6.7).[4] In 2003, 20 per cent of those aged 65–74 had consulted an NHS GP compared with 14 per cent in 1972. In part, the rise may be attributable to a number of recent initiatives that have been introduced to support older people to continue to live healthy independent lives. Among those aged 75 and over, the proportion has been fairly stable at around one in five. Since 1998, there has been an annual influenza immunisation campaign with the aim of reducing the serious morbidity and mortality due to flu. GPs offer free vaccinations to those people most likely to have a severe or complicated flu related illness, including all people aged 65 and over.[5] The *Chief Executive's Report to the NHS* indicated that in England there was an increase in flu injection uptake for people aged 65 and over, from 65 per cent in 2000 to 72 per cent in 2004.[6] Finally, free immunisation against pneumonia is offered to selected groups of older people. In 2004 it was offered to those aged 75 and over and the age limit will be lowered to 65 in 2005.

As well as a rise in consultations over time, there has also been a change in the site of these consultations. Consultations at home have fallen, while surgery visits and telephone consultations have risen. In 1971, 73 per cent of all NHS consultations were made at the surgery, health centre or elsewhere, whereas 22 per cent took place at home and just 4 per cent were by phone. By 2003, home visits had fallen to just

Figure **6.7**

NHS general practitioner consultations in previous 2 weeks: by age, 1972 to 2003[1]

Great Britain

Percentages

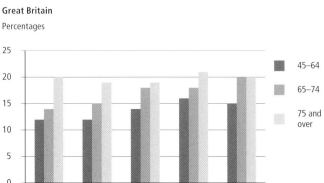

1 2001 onwards using weighted data.

Source: General Household Survey, Office for National Statistics

4 per cent, with phone consultations constituting 10 per cent and consultation at the surgery or elsewhere 86 per cent.[4]

Hospital services

Overall, one in five people aged 50 and over had attended an outpatient or casualty department in the three months prior to the interview. One in ten had stayed in hospital as an inpatient in the previous 12 months and 8 per cent had been a day patient in the last 12 months. Use of hospital services by people aged 50 and over varied by age, particularly outpatient and casualty attendances. For example, in 2002/03 the proportion increased from 16 per cent among 50–64 year-olds to 25 per cent among those 75 and over (Table 6.3). This may reflect the fact that older people are more likely to attend casualty due to an accident in the home than younger people.

Annually, there are approximately 2.7 million accidents in the home that require a hospital visit.[7] Falls constitute the main cause of these accidents, accounting for 40 per cent of the non-fatal injuries and 46 per cent of all deaths. There are 4,000 deaths from falls each year, of which nearly 80 per cent of the victims are aged 65 and over and only 5 per cent under the age of 40. Approximately 400,000 older people require hospital treatment for injuries sustained by falls.[8]

Not surprisingly, utilisation of hospital services was higher among older people with physical ill health, defined by the presence of a LLTI, than those without (Table 6.4). For example, among people aged 50–64 with a LLTI, 28 per cent had attended an outpatient or casualty department in the previous three months compared with just 11 per cent of those with no LLTI of the same age. A similar differential in health care use by morbidity was seen for hospital day patient and inpatient visits. Presence of mental health problems (CIS-R score of 12 and over) was also associated with a greater likelihood of an outpatient visit or inpatient stay (Table 6.5), particularly at ages 60–64 and 65–69. For example, among those aged 60–64, 49 per cent of those with a neurotic disorder had made an outpatient visit in the previous year compared with 19 per cent of those without.

Over time, there has been a marked increase in the proportion of older people reporting attendance at an outpatient or casualty department in the previous three months. In 1972, just 12 per cent of people aged 75 and over had attended as an outpatient, but in 2003 this was nearly double at 23 per cent (Figure 6.8). The proportions were similar across the age groups in the 1970s, but then widened as the proportion rose most sharply for the elderly from the mid-1980s onwards.

Figure **6.8**

Attendence at an outpatient or casualty department in the last 3 months: by age, 1972 to 2003[1]

Great Britain

Percentages

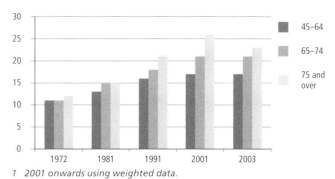

1 2001 onwards using weighted data.

Source: General Household Survey, Office for National Statistics

The proportions of older people reporting an inpatient stay have been relatively stable over the period since 1982 among younger age groups. Among those aged 75 and over, there was a rise in inpatient utilisation rates in the 1980s and early 1990s, from 13 per cent in 1982 to 20 per cent in 1995. Utilisation rates then stabilised at 17–18 per cent until 2002, after which there was a slight fall to 15 per cent in 2003 (Figure 6.9). There has however been a notable increase in day patient treatment, with day patient utilisation rates rising from 3 per cent of those aged 75 and over in 1992 to 12 per cent in 2003.

Recent administrative data on finished consultant episodes (FCEs) for NHS hospitals in England confirms the upward trend in day cases.[9] Moreover the share of all FCEs attributed to older people has been rising. In 1998/99 people aged 65 and over accounted

Figure **6.9**

Older people reporting an inpatient stay in the last 12 months: by age, 1982 to 2003[1]

Great Britain

Percentages

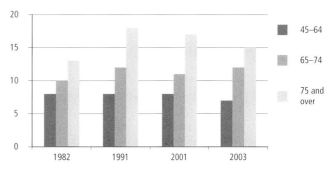

1 2001 onwards using weighted data.

Source: General Household Survey, Office for National Statistics

Figure **6.10**

Share of all finished consultant episodes in NHS hospitals: by age, 1998/99 and 2002/03

England
Percentages

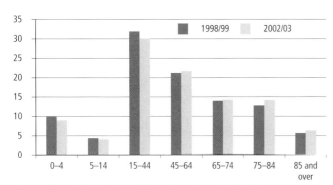

Source: Hospital Episode Statistics, Department of Health

for 33 per cent of all FCEs; by 2002/03 this had risen to 35 per cent (Figure 6.10). The overall number of FCEs also increased from 11.9 million in 1998/99 to 12.7 million in 2002/03.

Other health services

The pattern of use of other health services by people in later life varies according to the service being provided. The proportion reporting seeing a dentist in the last three months falls dramatically with age (Figure 6.11). This reflects the use of dentures among older people, particularly among those aged 75 and over. In contrast, the use of chiropody services increased with age, from 18 per cent of women aged 65–69 to 62 per cent among women aged 85 and over. Older women

were more likely to visit a chiropodist than older men (Figure 6.12). Older people living alone (most of whom are female) were more likely than those living with other people to access chiropody services, possibly reflecting the absence of another household member to help cut their toenails.[10] The pattern of utilisation of ophthalmic services was different again, without a clear gradient with age, varying from 13–19 per cent for men and 18–23 per cent among women (Figure 6.13). Since 1999, everyone aged 60 and over has been entitled to a free NHS sight test.

Figure **6.12**

People aged 65 and over who visited a chiropodist in the last 3 months, 2001/02[1]

Great Britain
Percentages

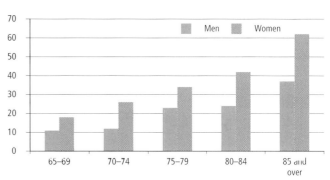

1 Using weighted data.

Source: Author's analysis using General Household Survey, Office for National Statistics

Figure **6.11**

People aged 65 and over who visited a dentist in the last 3 months, 2001/02[1]

Great Britain
Percentages

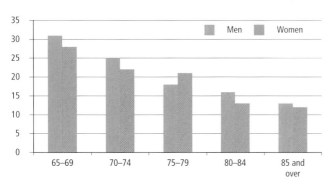

1 Using weighted data.

Source: Author's analysis using General Household Survey, Office for National Statistics

Figure **6.13**

People aged 65 and over who visited an optician in the last 3 months, 2001/02[1]

Great Britain
Percentages

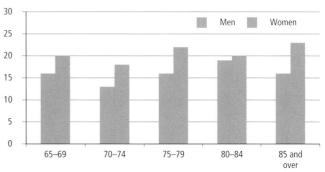

1 Using weighted data.

Source: Author's analysis using General Household Survey, Office for National Statistics

Residential care

According to the 2001 Census, there were approximately 450,000 people living in medical and care establishments in England and Wales. Of these, 341,000 (80 per cent) were aged 50 and over. Approximately 2 per cent of all people aged 50 and over were living in such communal establishments. Not surprisingly, this figure varied considerably with age, rising from 0.3 per cent among those aged 50–59 to 27 per cent among those aged 90 and over (Table 6.14). There were also significant differences by gender, with 29 per cent of women aged 90 and over and 14 per cent of those aged 85–89 resident in these establishments compared with 17 per cent and 8 per cent of men respectively. This reflects gender differentials in marital status, with older men being more likely than older women to have a living spouse, and hence the potential for someone to provide care and support.

Medical and care establishments refer to NHS psychiatric hospital/home and other hospital homes; local authority, private or voluntary residential or nursing care homes; housing association homes or hostels; and other psychiatric hospital/home, hospitals or medical and care homes.

The NHS Plan[11] and the National Service Framework for Older People[12] have continued the commitment of recent governments to support older people to live independently in their own homes. There has been a slight fall in the number of places in residential care homes for people aged 65 and over in England since 1994 from 247,000 to 237,000.[13] This is despite the fact that the total number of people aged 75 and over in England has increased from 3.4 million to 3.8 million.

Table **6.14**

People aged 50 and over living in medical and care establishments: by age and sex, April 2001

England and Wales   Percentages

	50–59	60–64	65–74	75–84	85–89	90 and over
Men						
All medical & care establishments	0.3	0.4	0.7	2.5	8.0	16.9
NHS[1]	0.1	0.1	0.1	0.1	0.2	0.3
Local authority	-	-	0.1	0.3	0.9	1.7
Nursing home	0.0	0.0	0.0	-	-	0.1
Residential care home	-	-	0.1	0.3	0.8	1.6
Other[2]	-	0.0	-	-	-	0.0
Housing association[3]	-	-	-	0.1	0.1	0.3
Private & voluntary	0.3	0.3	0.7	2.4	7.8	16.6
Nursing home	0.1	0.1	0.3	1.1	3.2	6.2
Residential care home	0.1	0.2	0.3	0.9	3.4	8.1
Other[4]	0.1	0.1	0.1	0.4	1.2	2.3
Women						
All medical & care establishments	0.2	0.3	0.8	4.3	14.3	29.4
NHS[1]	-	-	0.1	0.1	0.3	0.4
Local authority	-	-	0.1	0.5	1.5	3.1
Nursing home	0.0	0.0	0.0	-	0.1	0.1
Residential care home	-	0.0	0.1	0.4	1.4	2.9
Other[2]	0.0	-	-	-	-	-
Housing association[3]	-	-	-	0.1	0.2	0.5
Private & voluntary	0.2	0.3	0.7	3.6	12.3	25.4
Nursing home	0.1	0.1	0.3	1.6	5.1	10.3
Residential care home	0.1	0.1	0.3	1.9	6.9	14.6
Other[4]	-	-	-	0.1	0.3	0.5

1 Psychiatric hospital/home, other hospital home.
2 Other local authority home.
3 Housing association home or hostel.
4 Private/voluntary psychiatric hospital/home, medical and care home, hospital.

Source: Census 2001, Office for National Statistics

Figure **6.15**

Council supported residents aged 65 and over: by type of accommodation, 1994 to 2004

England
Thousands

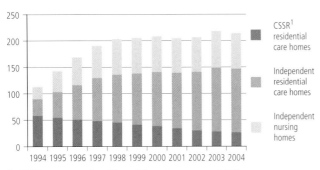

1   CSSRs are councils with social services responsibilities.

Source: Community Care Statistics, Department of Health

Figure **6.16**

Number of contact hours of home care: by sector[1], 1994 to 2004

England
Thousands

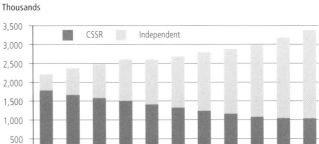

1   CSSRs are councils with social services responsibilities.

Source: Community Care Statistics, Department of Health

There has also been a shift in the type of provider of residential care for older people, with an increase in the number of places in private and voluntary homes and a fall in the number of local authority homes.[13] However, although places in council homes have fallen, the number of older residents supported (that is, financed) by councils in all types of residential homes has risen (Figure 6.15).

There was a significant increase in the number of older people in residential care homes supported by Councils with Social Services Responsibilities (CSSRs) over the period 1994–1998, reflecting the shift in responsibility for financial support from social security to local authorities as a result of the *1990 Community Care Act*.[14, 15] Between 1998 and 2002 the number was relatively stable at just over 200,000 but in 2003 there was an increase of 12,000 (6 per cent) on the previous year (Figure 6.15). Most of the increase has been in residents supported within the private and independent sector. In 2004 CSSR homes accounted for just 12 per cent of all supported residents aged 65 and over compared with 25 per cent in 1997 and 52 per cent in 1994.

Social services

As mentioned above, the majority of older people continue to live in the community well into later life. Even among those aged 90 and over, just under three quarters were living in private households in 2001. As stated in *Modernising Social Services*, the Government is committed to increasing the number of older people who are helped to continue living independently at home.[16]

The volume of home help hours purchased or provided by councils in England has increased significantly over the past two decades. In 2004 an estimated 3.4 million contact hours were provided to around 355,600 households, compared with 2.2 million hours in 1994.[17] Once more there is evidence of a change with respect to type of provider. In 2004 direct provision of home care accounted for just 31 per cent of all contact hours compared with 49 per cent in 1999 and 81 per cent in 1994 (Figure 6.16).

These figures do not take into account changes in the volume of people in need of care. Figure 6.17 shows both the total number of households in England receiving CSSR-funded home care and the number of households receiving home care services per 1,000 population aged 75 and over. Although the overall number of hours supplied has increased, the number of households receiving CSSR-funded home care services has fallen consistently since 1994 and the fall per 1,000 population aged 75 and over has been sharper than the general rate of decline. This suggests that councils are providing more intensive services for a smaller number of households. This is confirmed by the trends in the Department of Health *Community Care Statistics* regarding the intensity of home help/home care provision since 1994 (Figure 6.18). The proportion of client households receiving more than five hours of home help/home care contact and six or more visits has increased steadily from 15 per cent in 1994 to 46 per cent in 2004. Those receiving two hours or less of home help/home care and one visit has fallen from 34 per cent in 1994 to 13 per cent in 2004.

Figure **6.17**

Households receiving CSSR[1] funded home care/help: by household rate and total number of households, 1994 to 2004[2]

England

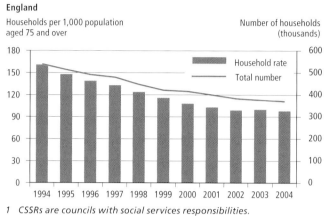

1 CSSRs are councils with social services responsibilities.
2 Prior to 2000 it was not possible to exclude double counting. For comparative purposes, the series including double counting in all years has been used.

Source: Community Care Statistics, Department of Health

Figure **6.18**

Intensity[1] of home help/home care, 1994 to 2004[2]

England

Percentages

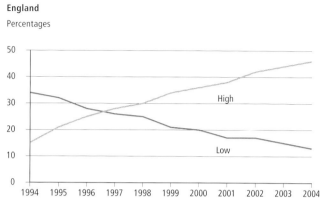

1 Low intensity is 1 visit and 2 hours or less. High intensity is 6 or more visits and more than 5 hours.
2 Survey week in each year.

Source: Community Care Statistics, Department of Health

Table **6.19**

Use of personal social services by people aged 65 and over living in the community: by age, 2001/02

Great Britain   Percentages

	65–69	70–74	75–79	80–84	85 and over
Local authority home help	1	2	3	7	18
Private home help	5	6	10	17	28
District nurse/health visitor	2	3	5	10	19
Day centre	1	2	2	5	9
Lunch club	1	3	4	5	7
Meals-on-wheels	0	0	1	4	7
Social worker	0	1	2	1	5
Voluntary organisation	1	1	1	2	4

Source: Author's analysis using General Household Survey, Office for National Statistics

Administrative data on the volume of home care supplied can be supplemented with analysis of receipt of care by older people using data from the General Household Survey. In 2001/02, 4 per cent of older people aged 65 and over living in a private household in Great Britain reported that they had used a home help or home care worker in the last month and 10 per cent reported that they had used private domestic help.

Six per cent had been visited by a nurse or health visitor in the last month, 3 per cent had used a day centre and 2 per cent had used meals on wheels. The proportion using personal social services increased with age, with nearly a fifth (18 per cent) of those aged 85 and over receiving local authority home help compared with just 1 per cent of those aged 65 to 69 (Table 6.19).

Table **6.20**

Use of personal social services in the previous month among people aged 65 and over[1]

Great Britain   Percentages

	1980	1985	1990/91	1994/95	2001/02
Home help (local authority)					
Men	4	6	6	5	3
Women	12	12	11	10	5
All	9	9	9	8	4
Home help (private)					
Men	..	..	4	5	9
Women	..	..	4	8	12
All	..	..	4	7	10
Meals-on-wheels					
Men	2	2	2	2	1
Women	3	3	3	3	2
All	2	2	3	3	2
District nurse/health visitor					
Men	4	4	4	4	4
Women	8	8	7	7	6
All	6	6	6	6	5

1 Unweighted data – analysis using weighted data for 2001/02 showed little difference in the results and overall trends. Information on the use of private home helps was not asked in 1980 and 1985.

Source: Evandrou and Falkingham (2005) (Reference 17), using General Household Survey, Office for National Statistics

Analysis of the GHS confirms the fall in the proportion of older people receiving local authority home help over time from 9 per cent of all men and women over 65 in 1980 to 4 per cent in 2001/02 (Table 6.20). At the same time there has been a rise in the proportion of older people reporting using a private home help from 4 per cent in 1990/91 to 10 per cent in 2001/02. There has been little change in the proportion receiving a visit from a district nurse or health visitor or receiving meals on wheels. This is despite the fact that there has been a change in the composition of the population aged 65 and over, with an increase in the very old who are likely to be in greatest need of services.

Taking 'need' into account, a different picture emerges. Table 6.21 shows the proportion of older people who used a personal social service in the last month *among* those who were unable to walk out of door unaided, by their household composition. Comparing Tables 6.20 and 6.21, receipt of services is higher among dependent older people, indicating that services are targeted to those individuals in greatest need. Service receipt is also higher among older people unable to walk out of doors unaided and living alone compared with

those living with others, although there has been a significant fall over time in public services. For example, receipt of local authority home care services has fallen from 45 per cent in 1994/95 to 28 per cent in 2001/02, and meals-on-wheels has fallen from 17 per cent to 12 per cent over the same period. This will have implications for the quality of life of older people continuing to live at home.

Informal care

Family members supply the majority of social care provided in the community. In 2001/02 over three-quarters (78 per cent) of all older people who reported suffering from mobility problems were helped by their spouse or other household members (Figure 6.22). Household members were also the main source of support for getting in and out of bed (74 per cent), walking down the road (60 per cent) and help in using public transport (63 per cent). Apart from getting in and out of bed, for which 12 per cent of respondents used services provided by the National Health Service or local authority social services, only a small proportion used help from anyone other than a household member or a relative living outside the household.

Table **6.21**

Use of personal social services in the previous month among people aged 65 and over: by functional capacity and living arrangements[1]

Great Britain   Percentages

	1980	1985	1994/95	2001/02
Percentage of people aged 65 and over unable to walk out of doors unaided	12	12	13	14
Of whom percentage in receipt of personal social service:				
Home help (local authority)				
Lives alone	62	55	45	28
Lives with others	15	17	15	8
Home help (private)				
Lives alone	..	..	19	32
Lives with others	..	..	6	10
Meals-on-wheels				
Lives alone	18	18	17	12
Lives with others	4	3	4	2
District nurse/health visitor				
Lives alone	33	30	30	27
Lives with others	24	18	18	19

1   Unweighted data – analysis using weighted data for 2001/02 showed little difference in the results and overall trends. Information on the use of private home helps was not asked in 1980 and 1985.

Source: Evandrou and Falkingham (2005) (Reference 17) using General Household Survey, Office for National Statistics

Table **6.22**

Sources of help with mobility tasks for people aged 65 and over, 2001/02[1]

Great Britain   Percentages

	Mobility	Getting in and out of bed	Walking down the road	Using public transport
Spouse or partner	58	60	43	52
Other household member	20	14	17	11
Non-household relative	8	4	19	16
Friend/neighbour	4	2	14	7
NHS or personal social services	4	12	1	1
Paid help	2	5	2	4
Other household member	5	2	4	8

1   Using weighted data.

Source: Author's analysis using General Household Survey, Office for National Statistics

Table **6.23**

Sources of help with self-care and domestic tasks among people aged 65 and over: by whether living alone or with spouse, 2001/02[1]

Great Britain

Percentages

	Cutting toenails	Bathing/ Washing	Domestic tasks	Personal affairs	Cooking	Shopping
a) Living alone						
Non-household relative	8	38	48	86	36	65
Friend/neighbour	1	9	15	7	5	18
NHS or personal social services	2	32	4	3	24	7
Paid help	1	13	25	1	14	8
Chiropodist	86	.	.	.	.	.
Other	1	8	5	2	15	3
Nobody	-	-	2	1	5	-
Total	100	100	100	100	100	100
b) Living with spouse						
Spouse or partner	32	87	69	98	93	88
Non-household relative	4	7	14	2	2	8
Friend/neighbour	-	-	2	-	-	2
NHS or personal social services	2	6	1	-	1	1
Paid help	-	-	11	-	3	2
Chiropodist	60	.	.	.	.	.
Other	2	-	2	-	-	-
Nobody	-	-	1	-	1	-
Total	100	100	100	100	100	100

1 Using weighted data.

Source: Author's analysis using General Household Survey, Office for National Statistics

There is a strong relationship between an older person's living arrangements and use of formal services to provide assistance with self-care and domestic tasks (Table 6.23) Older people living alone were significantly more likely to use a local authority home help or private domestic help than those living with other household members. Among those older people who were unable to bathe or wash unaided, 32 per cent of those who live alone reported receiving assistance from the NHS or personal social services compared with just 6 per cent living with others. Where older people live with others, household members are the main source of support and even among those living alone, the majority receive support from non-household relatives or friends.

As well as receiving informal care, older people are also major providers of care. In 2001, 1.2 million men and 1.6 million women aged 50 and over in England and Wales were providing unpaid care to family members, neighbours or relatives (Table

6.24). This represents 16 per cent of men aged 50 and over and 17 per cent of women. Around a quarter of older informal carers are providing 50 or more hours of unpaid care a week. This proportion increases with age. For those aged 85 and over, around half of those providing care did so for 50 or more hours a week.

The proportion of older people providing care declines with age. For example, 25 per cent of women aged 50–54 provided care compared with 20 per cent of those aged 60–64 and just 3 per cent of women aged 85 and over (Table 6.25). Among 50–64 year olds, a greater proportion of women than men provide unpaid care, and a higher proportion provide intensive care (50 or more hours a week). However for the older age groups (75 and over), men are more likely to provide care than women, and are more likely to be providing intensive care. For example, 4 per cent of men aged 85 and over reported providing 50 or more hours a week of unpaid care compared with 1 per cent of women of the same age.

Table 6.24

Provision of unpaid care[1] by people aged 50 and over: by age and sex, April 2001

England and Wales   Thousands/Percentages

	Number providing care (thousands)		Percentage of carers providing 50 or more hours a week	
	Men	Women	Men	Women
50–54	311	446	14	16
55–59	268	365	16	19
60–64	203	262	21	25
65–74	291	334	31	33
75–84	144	137	44	43
85 and over	23	19	54	47
All	1,239	1,563	24	25

1 Individuals providing unpaid care to family members, neighbours or relatives.

Source: Census 2001, **Office for National Statistics**

Table 6.25

Provision of unpaid care[1] by people aged 50 and over: by age, sex and number of hours a week, April 2001

England and Wales   Percentages

	50–54	55–59	60–64	65–74	75–84	85 and over	All aged 50 and over
Men							
1–19 hours	13	14	11	8	5	3	10
20–49 hours	2	2	2	2	2	1	2
50 or more hours	3	3	3	4	5	4	4
Does not provide care	83	82	84	86	88	92	85
Women							
1–19 hours	18	17	13	8	4	1	11
20–49 hours	3	3	2	2	1	-	2
50 or more hours	4	5	5	5	3	1	4
Does not provide care	75	76	80	86	92	97	83

1 Individuals providing unpaid care to family members, neighbours or relatives.

Source: Census 2001, **Office for National Statistics**

Older people from White British backgrounds are more likely to be providing informal care to relatives, friends or neighbours (15 per cent) compared with those from Indian (13 per cent), Bangladeshi (12 per cent), Black Caribbean (11 per cent) and Chinese (9 per cent) ethnic groups (Figure 6.26). This in part reflects differences in age structure, with minority ethnic groups being much younger than the White population and

less likely to have frail family members in need of care. However, among those aged 55 and over who provide care, a higher proportion of Bangladeshis and Pakistanis provide informal care for 50 or more hours a week than their counterparts from other minority ethnic groups or the White British ethnic group (Figure 6.27).

References

1 Department of Health (2004) *Departmental Report* 2004, TSO: London.

2 Evans O, Singleton N, Meltzer H, Stewart R and Prince M (2003) *The Mental Health of Older People*, TSO: London.

3 Lewis G and Pelosi A (1990) *Manual of revised clinical interview schedule (CIS-R)*, Institute of Psychiatry: London.

4 Office for National Statistics (2004) *Living in Britain: Results from the 2002 General Household Survey*, TSO: London.

5 Department of Health (2005) *Flu.* Policy and guidance. http://www.dh.gov.uk/PolicyAndGuidance/HealthAndSocialCareTopics/Flu/fs/en

6 Department of Health (2005) *Chief Executive's Report to the NHS: Statistical Supplement May 2005*, Department of Health: London. http://www.dh.gov.uk/assetRoot/04/11/04/16/04110416.pdf

7 Department of Trade and Industry (1999) *Avoiding Slips, Trips and Broken Hips: Accidental Falls in the Home. Regional Distribution of Cases Involving People Aged over 65 in the UK*, Health Education Authority: London. http://www.dti.gov.uk/homesafetynetwork/pdffalls/stats.pdf

8 Department of Health (2004) *Better Health in Old Age*, Report from Prof Ian Philp, Department of Health: London. http://www.dh.gov.uk/assetRoot/04/09/32/15/04093215.pdf

9 Hospital Episode Statistics produced by the Health & Social Care. Information Centrethe Department of Health. http://www.dh.gov.uk/PublicationsAndStatistics/Statistics/HospitalEpisodeStatistics/fs/enhttp://www.hesonline.org.uk

10 Office for National Statistics (2003) *People aged 65 and over: results of a study carried out on behalf of the Department of Health as part of the 2001 General Household Survey*, TSO: London.

11 Department of Health (2000) *The NHS Plan*, TSO: London.

12 Department of Health (2001) *National Service Framework for Older People*, Department of Health: London.

13 Department of Health (2005) *Community Care Statistics 2004: Supported Residents*, Department of Health: London.

Figure **6.26**

People aged 55 and over providing unpaid care: by ethnic group and number of hours caring, April 2001

England and Wales
Percentages

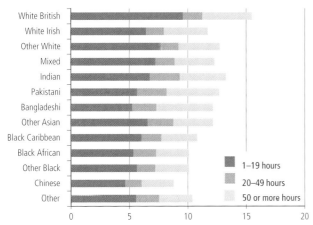

Source: Census 2001, Office for National Statistics

Figure **6.27**

Carers aged 55 and over providing 50 or more hours a week: by ethnic group, April 2001

England and Wales
Percentages

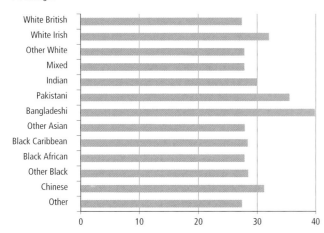

Source: Census 2001, Office for National Statistics

14 Evandrou M and Falkingham J (1998) The personal social services, in H Glennerster H and J Hills J (eds) *The State of Welfare*, 2nd edition. Oxford University Press, Oxford, pp.189–256.

15 Evandrou M and Falkingham J (2005) A Secure Retirement for All? Older People and New Labour, in Hills J and Stewart K (eds) *A More Equal Society? New Labour, Poverty, Inequality and Exclusion*, Polity Press: Bristol.

16 Department of Health (1998) *Modernising Social Services: Promoting independence, improving protection, raising standards.* Cm **4169**. TSO: London.

17 Department of Health (2005) *Community Care Statistics 2004: Home Care Services for Adults, England*, Department of Health: London.

Income, wealth and expenditure

Stephen Balchin and A Soule
Department for Work and Pensions

Chapter 7

Key findings

- As people get older the sources of their income change. Households where the household reference person is aged 50–59 get over 80 per cent of their income from employment and self-employment, while for those aged 70–79, 50 per cent of their income is from the State Pension and other benefits, and 33 per cent from private pensions

- Income in retirement reflects decisions taken during a pensioners' working life - people with broken work records are less likely to have built up rights to high levels of pensions. Married female pensioners had an average income (in their own right) of £77 per week in 2003/04, compared with married male pensioners who have an average income (in their own right) of £212 per week

- From the mid-1990s pensioners' incomes rose faster than average earnings. This was a result of both increased state benefits, and of the increased coverage and value of private pensions

- A substantial proportion of older people have access to wealth or assets of some form. Older people aged 60–64 had a median financial and physical wealth of £25,000 in 2003/04

- Spending patterns change as people get older, with an increasing share going on food, housing and fuel: where the household reference person was aged 50–59, 10 per cent of spending was on food in 2003/04, compared with 15 per cent where the household reference person was aged 80 or over

Introduction

This chapter looks at the financial resources of older people: their income, their wealth (including savings and other assets), and how they use these resources. Income allows people to access the goods and services which determine their material standard of living, and allows them to take part in society more widely. It refers to a flow of monetary resources over a period; older people's incomes come from a range of sources including employment, the state retirement pension, other state benefits, and private pensions. Some measures of income include income in kind, such as free TV licences to those over 75. Wealth refers to an asset valued at a specific period of time and can include savings, stocks and shares, pension funds, and property.

Levels and sources of income

As people get older they tend to retire from paid work, and so their main sources of income shift from employment and self-employment to state and private pensions and other benefits. Table 7.1 shows the proportion of household income from different sources. The proportion of income from employment and self-employment falls from over 80 per cent for households headed by someone aged 50–59, to 10 per cent for households headed by someone aged 70–79. As the proportion of income from employment and self-employment falls an increasing proportion comes from the state pension and other state benefits.

Along with this shift in the sources of income, the level of income older people receive also falls. The median net household income for people over 80 is £232 a week, compared with £353 for people aged 50–59 (after housing costs, and equivalised in order to adjust for household size) (Figure 7.2).

Figure **7.2**

Median weekly equivalised household income[1]: by age, 2003/04

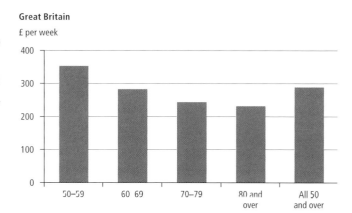

Great Britain

£ per week

1 Median household equivalised income, on an after housing costs basis.

Source: Family Resources Survey, Department for Work and Pensions

Pensioners' incomes

People retire from the labour market at a range of different ages (as detailed in Chapter 4). This section looks at incomes of those above State Pension Age (SPA), the age when people are entitled to the state pension (60 for women, and 65 for men). Here the SPA is a convenient way of dividing the population of older people into those who are likely to be in work, and those who are not. This section gives a brief overview of the different sources of income that pensioners receive. It is, necessarily, a simplified overview. The further reading section at the end of this chapter lists publications that give more detail on state benefits, and the private pension system.

For people over SPA, the State Pension is the most common source of income. The State Pension is a contributory benefit, based on National Insurance Contributions paid through

Table **7.1**

Components of weekly household income: by age of head of household, 2003/04

Great Britain

Percentages

	Wages and salaries	Self employment income	Investments	State Pension plus any MIG/Pension Credit	Private pensions	Social security benefits and other sources	Sample size (=100%)
50–59	69	12	3	1	7	8	5,118
60–69	32	8	5	19	25	11	4,287
70–79	7	3	6	40	33	12	3,712
80 and over	4	1	6	44	26	20	1,957

Source: Family Resources Survey, Department for Work and Pensions

someone's working life. There are also provisions to protect entitlements of those who don't work because they are caring for children, or for a person who was ill or disabled. The State Pension is made up of the Basic State Pension, and an additional pension: the State Second Pension (or S2P), which replaced the State Earnings Related Pension (SERPS) in 2002. The additional pension provides a top up based on earnings, although people can 'contract-out' of the additional pension, paying lower National Insurance Contributions, if they are contributing to a private scheme.

Almost all pensioners receive income from the State Pension (99 per cent of couples and 98 per cent of single pensioners). According to the Pensioners' Incomes Series (based on the Family Resources Survey) on average, single pensioners received £90 from the State Pension in 2003/04 and pensioner couples received £149. The average income from the State Pensions has increased in real terms by 15 per cent since 1994/95.

Pensioners are often eligible for other state benefits. Broadly these fall into two categories: income-related and disability-related benefits. Income-related benefits include Pension Credit, Housing Benefit and Council Tax Benefit. Pension Credit (which replaced Minimum Income Guarantee in 2003) provides an income top up for low and moderate income pensioners. Housing Benefit and Council Tax Benefit provide help with the costs of rent and Council Tax. The proportion of pensioners receiving these income-related benefits has fallen over the last nine years. Forty per cent of single pensioners were in receipt of income-related benefits in 2003/04, compared with 47 per cent in 1994/95. Similarly, 17 per cent of pensioner couples were in receipt in 2003/04, down from 24 per cent in 1994/95. Although the proportions receiving such benefits have fallen, the amount typically received has risen in real terms: from £24 per head for pensioner couples in 1994/95 to £41 per head in

Figure **7.3**

Median amount of income–related benefits for those in receipt, 1994/95 and 2003/04

Great Britain

£ per week

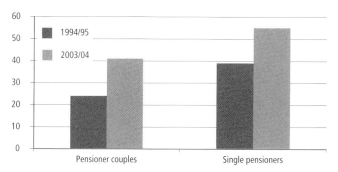

Source: Family Resources Survey, Department for Work and Pensions

2003/04 (Figure 7.3). For single pensioners the amount rose from £39 per head to £55 per head over the period.

Single pensioners were about twice as likely as pensioners living in a couple to be in receipt of income-related benefits. These benefits were also more common among older pensioners, who on average have less private income. However, take up estimates of income-related benefits published by the Department for Work and Pensions have shown that there was lower take up of income-related benefits by older people.[1] Research identified the main barriers to claiming benefits as a lack of awareness about the eligibility criteria for the benefits they were entitled to, or a belief that they could manage without claiming.[2,3]

Disability-related benefits include Disability Living Allowance and Attendance Allowance which provide a contribution towards the costs of disability. These benefits are paid in addition to any other income or savings that someone has. Disability benefits are usually paid at one of a number of rates. For example, in 2003/04 Attendance Allowance was paid at either a lower rate (£38.30 per week) or a higher rate (£57.20 per week), depending on how much a recipient's disability affected them. Those claiming Attendance Allowance or Disability Living Allowance can also claim higher amounts of income-related benefits (Pension Credit, Housing Benefit and Council Tax Benefit). In 2003/04, 24 per cent of pensioner couples, and 22 per cent of single pensioners received some form of disability benefit.

In addition to state benefits most pensioners have some form of private income: 81 per cent of single pensioners and 93 per cent of pensioner couples have income on top of state benefits. This may be in the form of earnings, investments, or private pensions.

Occupational pensions, provided by a former employer, are the most common form of private pension. In 2003/04, 73 per cent of pensioner couples, and 55 per cent of single pensioners received an occupational pension (Figure 7.4 – see overleaf). The proportion of pensioners in receipt of occupational pensions grew in the 1980s, but has been more stable in the 1990s. The rise was particularly pronounced for single pensioners: from 29 per cent in 1979 the proportion receiving occupational pensions almost doubled by 2003/04. The growth in receipt of occupational pensions through the 1980s has mostly been due to the rapid increase in the coverage of these schemes in the 1950s and 1960s.

Personal pensions are the other form of private pensions. These are arrangements between an individual and a pension or insurance company, and may be employer-sponsored or set up independently by the individual. Data from the Family Resources

Figure **7.4**

Proportion of pensioner units[1] in receipt of occupational pension income, 1979 to 2003/04

United Kingdom/Great Britain

Percentages

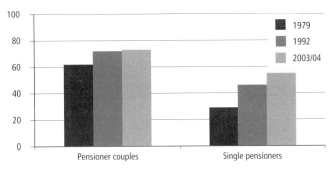

1 *A pensioner unit is defined as either a single person over State Pension Age, or a couple where the man is over State Pension Age.*

Source: Family Expenditure Survey, Office for National Statistics; Family Resources Survey, Department for Work and Pensions

Survey on the amount and source of income are self-reported and so can be subject to misreporting. In particular, widows who have inherited pension rights may not know whether the income is from an occupational pension, a personal pension or is an annuity from some other form of investment.

Personal pensions were only introduced in 1988. The proportion of pensioners receiving income from personal pensions has increased in recent years, but it is still the case that only a small proportion of pensioners receive personal pension income: 18 per cent of pensioner couples, and 6 per cent of single pensioners in 2003/04 (Figure 7.5). As the proportion of people with personal pensions is increasing, younger pensioners are more likely to have personal pensions.

Figure **7.5**

Pensioner units[1] in receipt of personal pension income, 1994/95 and 2003/04

Great Britain

Percentages

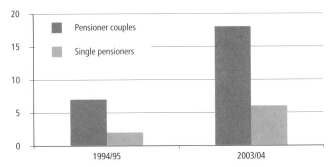

1 *A pensioner unit is defined as either a single person over State Pension Age, or a couple where the man is over State Pension Age.*

Source: Family Resources Survey, Department for Work and Pensions

Investment income includes income from other forms of private investment, for example stocks and shares, or savings accounts. This section covers income from investments specifically, rather than the stock of investments which is covered in the section on wealth. Most pensioners have some form of investment income – 79 per cent of couples and 67 per cent of single pensioners. These proportions have changed little since 1994/95. Most pensioners receive a modest amount. For example, half of single pensioners with investment income receive £2 or less a week. However, there are a small number of pensioners with large amounts of investment income which means that the average (mean) is much higher. Figure 7.6 shows the mean and median investment income for those pensioners who receive this sort of income. The level of investment income varies from year to year much more than other sources of pensioners' incomes, as it depends not only on past choices but is also affected by changes in interest rates, and movements in the stockmarket.

Why pensioners have different levels of income

There are variations between the incomes of different groups of pensioners, although these variations are not as great as those in the incomes of families headed by someone below State Pension Age (SPA). A number of groups of people over SPA are more likely to have low levels of income in comparison with other pensioners: older pensioners, single pensioners, women and some ethnic minority groups (see Chapter 1 for more information on the older population by ethnic group). Wealth will be covered later in this chapter, but many of the causes of variation in pensioners' incomes also cause variation in their levels of wealth.

Figure **7.6**

Median and mean investment income for pensioner units[1], 2003/04

Great Britain

£ per week

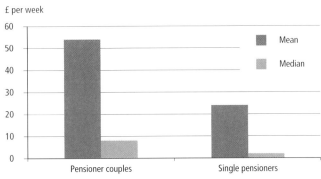

1 *A pensioner unit is defined as either a single person over State Pension Age, or a couple where the man is over State Pension Age.*

Source: Family Resources Survey, Department for Work and Pensions

Differences in pensioners' incomes usually reflect experiences over their working lives. In particular people with broken work records are less likely to have accrued rights to private pensions, or state second pensions. Women who have taken time off to care for children are likely to be affected by this. Some ethnic minority pensioners, who migrated to the UK late in their lives, will also have had less chance to accrue pension rights.

Pensioners' incomes will also be affected by birth cohort effects, which would be expected to change from one generation to another. For example, the current Government introduced the State Second Pension (S2P) in 2002 which makes better provision for women and carers. People have only been accruing rights to S2P since 2002, and so future cohorts will be more likely to receive this. More recent generations are also more likely to be home owners, and so are less likely to receive Housing Benefit.

Incomes of different groups

Different age groups

Younger pensioners on average retire with higher incomes from private pensions and investments than existing pensioners, whose incomes are fixed in real terms. Earnings tend to rise faster than prices, and so newly retired pensioners with salary-related private pensions will generally receive a higher pension than someone in an equivalent job who retired several years earlier, and whose incomes are often fixed in real terms.

Younger pensioners are also more likely to have income from some form of paid work, which makes up a large proportion of

Figure 7.7

Mean gross income of pensioner couples[1] and single pensioners: by age, 2003/04

Great Britain

£ per week

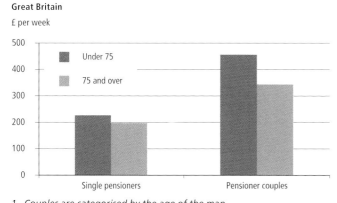

1 Couples are categorised by the age of the man.

Source: Family Resources Survey, Department for Work and Pensions

the difference in income between younger and older pensioners: 53 per cent of people aged 60–64 years and 18 per cent of those aged 65–69 were still in employment.

Figure 7.7 shows that older pensioners have lower incomes on average than those under 75 years. The average gross income for single pensioners aged 75 and over is £198 per week compared with £227 for single pensioners under 75. The difference is larger for pensioner couples: couples where the man is under 75 have an average income of £456 a week, whereas couples where the man is over 75 have an average income of £344 a week.

Couples and singles

Unsurprisingly pensioner couples have higher average incomes than single pensioners. Because men have lower life expectancies than women, single pensioners are more likely to be older, and female. Even when comparing the same age groups, pensioner couples on average have over twice as much investment and private pension income than single pensioners. Figure 7.7 shows that pensioner couples where the man is under 75 have over twice as much gross income as single pensioners in the same age group. (Results based on equivalised income can be sensitive to the exact equivalisation factors used; because of this equivalised income has not been used to compare couples and single pensioners).

Gender and marital status

So far this chapter has looked at the income of the household, or benefit unit. This section looks at the incomes of individual pensioners in order to explore the difference between the incomes of men and women.

Female pensioners on average have lower incomes than men, which is a result of a number of factors:

- women have had lower employment rates, partly because they are more likely to have taken on caring responsibilities and so are likely to have built up lower entitlements to state and private pensions;

- women in employment have had lower average earnings, and may either have built up lower pension funds or may not even have been eligible to be a member of an employers' pension scheme (a European Court of Justice ruling in May 1995 made it illegal for pension schemes to exclude part-time workers); and

- in the past married women were able to pay a reduced rate of National Insurance, which did not earn them an entitlement to the state pension in their own right.

In 2003/04 the median total individual income for retired men was higher than that for retired women (Figure 7.8). The difference was greatest for married pensioners: married men had a median income of £212 per week in their own right as opposed to £77 per week for married women. For single pensioners who had never been married, men and women had around the same median total income. Male divorcee and widower pensioners had higher incomes than female pensioners in the same categories, but the differences were much smaller than for married pensioners. For widowed pensioners this is because many women will have inherited some of their husband's pension rights.

Figure **7.8**

Median total individual income: by marital status and sex, 2003/04

Great Britain

£ per week

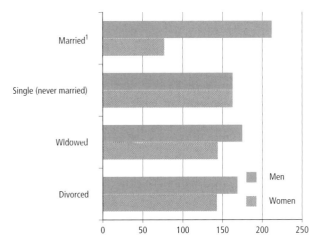

1 Married men and women are included if at least one member is over State Pension Age.
Source: Family Resources Survey, Department for Work and Pensions

Pensioners from ethnic minorities

A very small proportion of the older population aged 50 and over in the United Kingdom are from ethnic minority groups, which tend to have much younger age structures than the White population (see Chapter 1: Demographic profile for more information).

The sample sizes for ethnic minority pensioner groups on most sample surveys, including the Family Resources Survey, are small and so robust data are not available for some ethnic minority pensioner groups (for example Chinese), or for a finer break down of the groups.

Ethnic minority pensioners have, on average, lower incomes than White pensioners. This reflects lower average earnings among the ethnic minority population, and that some immigrants came to the UK part of the way through their

working lives, and so have had less time to build up pension rights in either state or private pensions.[4] In particular ethnic minority pensioners have lower average incomes from private pensions and investments. White pensioners had almost twice as much private pension income as Black or Asian pensioners in the three years 2001/02 to 2003/04 (Table 7.9). Income from state pensions and benefits was the largest source for all ethnic groups.

Table **7.9**

Gross incomes of pensioner units: by ethnic group, 2001–04[1]

Great Britain				£ per week at 2003/04 prices
	White	Asian/ Asian British	Black/ Black British	All
Gross income	285	217	220	283
of which:				
Benefit income	145	132	142	145
Occupational pension	75	31	42	74
Personal pension income	8	5	2	7
Investment income	26	16	7	26
Earnings	24	29	22	25
Other income	3	2	3	3

1 This table is based on data from 2001/02, 2002/03 and 2003/04 uprated to 2003/04 prices; results should be treated with caution. Results for Mixed, Chinese, and Other ethnic groups have not been given separately as they are based on particularly small sample sizes and have large margins of uncertainty.
Source: Family Resources Survey, Department for Work and Pensions

Research has shown that attitudes towards saving and provision in old age can be very different in different ethnic groups.[5] A study of Pakistani, Bangladeshi and White men in Oldham showed that among Bangladeshis and Pakistanis, low wages and financial responsibilities towards family and community meant that providing for retirement was a very low priority.

Early retirees

According to the Department for Work and Pensions (DWP) research, those who had retired voluntarily before the State Pension Age (SPA), had higher average incomes than people who retired at SPA (£256 per week compared with £196), with private pension income as the largest single component (Table 7.10).[6] In contrast people forced to retire early (through, for example, ill health or redundancy) had lower average incomes than those who retired at SPA (£186 per week compared with £196). Research also shows that spending falls sharply around retirement for those who are forced to retire, but for those who retire voluntarily spending declines far more smoothly over retirement, reflecting the unplanned nature of forced early retirement.[7]

Table **7.10**

Income and sources of income: by retirement status[1], 2002

Great Britain   £ per week/Percentages

	Retired early			Retired at SPA or later		
	Voluntary	Forced	Total	Retired at SPA	Retired Late	Total
Mean weekly benefit unit income	256	186	217	196	158	206
Percentage from earnings	9	13	12	6	6	9
Percentage from benefits (excludes state pension)	11	44	27	15	9	23
Percentage from state pension	30	22	26	55	61	36
Percentage from private pension	36	16	26	18	20	23
Percentage from other	14	5	10	6	4	8

1 Results for people who say they are fully retired from a sample of 50 to 69 year olds.

Source: Department for Work and Pensions (Reference 6)

Income distribution

This section looks at pensioners' position in the overall income distribution, and at pensioners below low income thresholds. Household incomes have been 'equivalised', that is adjusted to reflect the number of people in a household, allowing the comparison of incomes for households with different sizes and compositions. The results comparing single people with couples can be sensitive to the assumptions within this equivalisation process.

When looking at the income distribution, households are ranked by their net income. The DWP publication, *Households Below Average Incomes* (HBAI) provides statistics based on the net income distributions both before and after deducting housing costs. Whether incomes are measured on a before or after housing costs basis can have a significant impact on the position of pensioners in the income distribution.

About three quarters of pensioners are owner occupiers, with around two thirds owning their home outright. These pensioners will face lower housing costs than most non-pensioners and so will be better off if income after housing costs is the measure used. This section sets out results mainly using the income after housing costs measure – statistics on both bases are available from HBAI.

Pensioners are most likely to be in the second lowest quintile of the income distribution: 32 per cent were in quintile two in 2003/04, while just under 30 per cent were in quintiles four and five (Figure 7.11) (see the Glossary on page 80 for an explanation of quintiles). This contrasts with working-age adults who are most likely to be in the top two quintiles – nearly a half (47 per cent) in 2003/04.

Figure **7.11**

Income distribution[1]: by pensioners and working-age adults[2], 2003/04

Great Britain

Percentages

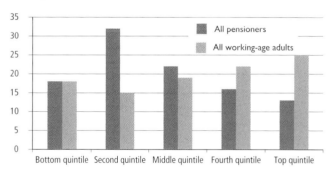

1 Distribution based on the net equivalised income on an after housing costs basis. Income distribution also includes children who are not shown in this figure.
2 Working-age adults are defined as those aged 20 and over, and under State Pension Age (60 for women and 65 for men).

Source: Households Below Average Income, Department for Work and Pensions

Low income

Low income can be measured in a number of ways. The Government's *Opportunity for All* indicators use income thresholds of 50, 60 and 70 per cent of median equivalised household income to define low income. The 60 per cent threshold of median income is most commonly used. For the rest of this section 'low income' will be defined as 'below 60 per cent of equivalised household median income', and the after housing costs figures will normally be quoted. Numbers below low incomes thresholds are often used as indicators of poverty. This is not the only way to approach poverty measurement, for example material deprivation measures look at the numbers who cannot afford a set of basic goods and services.

Older age groups have higher proportions below low income thresholds. Fifteen per cent of families without children headed by someone aged 50–54 years old have a low income, rising to 19 per cent of families headed by someone aged 55 and over, and 20 per cent of those over State Pension Age.

On an after housing costs basis the proportion of pensioners on a low income (20 per cent) is similar to that for all people (21 per cent) and the working-age population (19 per cent) (Figure 7.12). The difference is much larger on a before housing cost basis: 21 per cent of pensioners are on low incomes compared with 14 per cent of working-age adults. The smaller difference on an after housing cost basis is due to the higher level of owner occupation among pensioners, and their consequently low levels of housing costs. The difference between the after housing cost and before housing costs measures has narrowed over the last few years. This is partly due to the increasing proportion of pensioners who own their home outright. About two thirds of pensioners live in houses that are owned outright.

Some groups are more likely than others to have low incomes, or to be at the bottom of the income distribution. These groups include:

• Ethnic minority pensioners: 29 per cent were on low incomes in 2003/04, compared with 19 per cent of White pensioners.

• Single women: 21 per cent of single women are on low incomes, compared with 14 per cent of single men.

• Older pensioners: 23 per cent of single women over 75 were on low incomes, compared with 19 per cent of single women pensioners under 70.

Pensioners' incomes tend to be fixed in real terms (that is they increase with inflation). Because of this pensioners on low income are more likely than other groups to remain so. British Household Panel Survey data show that 23 per cent of pensioners on low income in one year will leave low income in the next – a lower 'exit rate' than any other group.[8] Sixty one per cent of the exits from low income for pensioners are associated with rises in benefit income.

International comparisons

As well as being one of the *Opportunity for All* indicators, the proportion of pensioners below 60 per cent of median income was also adopted by the Laeken European Council in December 2001 as one of a set of 18 statistical indicators for social inclusion.[9]

In 2001, the UK had the fifth highest rate of low income for people aged 65 and over on a before housing costs basis out of the EU countries (Figure 7.13). The UK rate at 25 per cent was 14 and 10 percentage points higher than France and Germany, respectively, but similar to Belgium, Austria and Denmark. Ireland had the highest proportion of people over 65 in low income at 44 per cent.

Figure **7.12**

People living in households with income[1] below 60 per cent of median, 1994/95 to 2003/04

Great Britain

Percentages

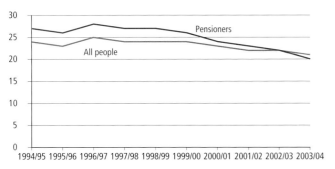

1 Based on equivalised net household income on an after housing cost basis.

Source: Households Below Average Income, Department for Work and Pensions

Figure **7.13**

People aged 65 and over with income[1] below 60 per cent of the national median, 2001

Percentages

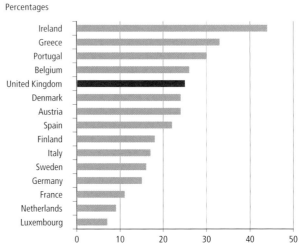

1 Based on equivalised household income on a before housing cost basis.

Source: Eurostat

Changes in incomes over time

Among older people incomes have risen consistently since the mid-1990s. For pensioners, net income after housing costs rose faster than net income before housing costs: the after housing costs measure increased by 38 per cent between 1995/96 and 2003/04 in real terms, compared with 28 per cent before housing costs (Figure 7.14). The growth in pensioner incomes over the period resulted from substantial increases in income from occupational pensions and benefits.

Figure 7.14

Pensioners' incomes[1,2]

United Kingdom/Great Britain

£ per week at 2003/04 prices

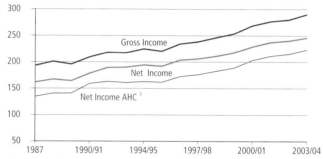

1 Based on benefit unit income levels either for single pensioners or pensioner couples.
2 Data for years up to and including 1993 is from the Family Expenditure Survey (United Kingdom), for 1994/95 onwards the Family Resources Survey (Great Britain) is used.
3 AHC - after housing costs.

Source: Family Expenditure Survey, Office for National Statistics, Family Resources Survey, Department for Work and Pensions

Figure 7.15

Pensioners' perception of how well they are managing financially[1], 2003/04

United Kingdom

Percentages

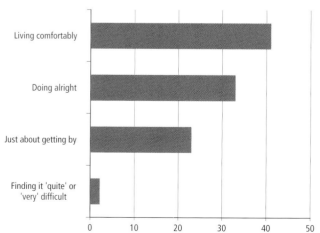

1 Respondents over SPA were asked the question 'How well would you say you yourself are managing financially these days'?

Source: British Household Panel Survey, Institute for Social and Economic Research

Satisfaction with incomes

It can be difficult to assess pensioners' perceptions of their own income. Research has shown that pensioners can place a high value on being seen to manage without support, and so may be unwilling to admit to experiencing hardship.[10-12] One study noted that although the pensioners interviewed were certainly in poverty 'no one complained about their situation'.[10]

Figure 7.15 shows pensioners responses to being asked how well they felt they were managing financially. A large proportion, 41 per cent, felt that they were living comfortably in retirement. A small percentage, 2 per cent, said they were finding it difficult to manage financially in retirement.

Those who had retired voluntarily before State Pension Age saw themselves financially better off in retirement (Table 7.16 – see overleaf). This was mainly due to the fact that people who retired voluntarily had the highest average income; they were also less likely than any other group to view themselves financially worse off since retirement. Those forced to retire early were most likely (along with those retiring late) to view themselves worse off than before their retirement.

According to a study commissioned by the Department for Work and Pensions on expectations and satisfaction of those who had retired, 44 per cent expressed the view that they were about as well off as they had expected.[13] Seventeen per cent said they were better-off and 38 per cent said that they were worse off. Over half (56 per cent) said that they were worse off when compared with the years before they retired, reflecting the pattern noted earlier where people's incomes were more likely to have fallen than risen on retirement.

Wealth

Income provides only a partial picture of the financial resources that are available to older people. Older people are more likely than other age groups to have built up a stock of wealth of some form which can act as a safety net. However, research shows that older people, especially older pensioners, can be reluctant to use up their savings.[14]

Wealth may come in a number of forms, some of which are easier to access than others. The English Longitudinal Study of Ageing – from which much of the data in this section comes – measures wealth under four headings:

- Financial wealth – including savings accounts and stocks and shares

- Physical wealth – which includes the value of second houses, and business assets the self employed may own, less the value of any debts secured against these assets

Table **7.16**

Whether financially better or worse off in retirement: by retirement status, 2002

Great Britain

Percentages

	Retired early			Retired at SPA and after		
	Voluntary	Forced	Total	Retired at SPA	Retired late	Total
Overall would you say you are financially better off, worse off or about the same in retirement compared to what you expected?						
Better off	25	11	18	17	13	17
Worse off	20	56	39	34	41	38
About the same	53	32	42	48	46	44
Overall would you say you are financially better off, worse off or about the same compared to the years just before retirement?						
Better off	20	9	14	16	7	14
Worse off	46	68	58	48	68	56
About the same	33	23	28	36	25	29

Source: Department for Work and Pensions

- Housing wealth – the value of someone's house, less any debts secured against it

- Pension wealth – the value of the accrued rights to pensions, whether state, occupational or personal

It is difficult to estimate pension wealth with existing sources because assumptions have to be made about past work history, and what rights to pensions someone has accrued.[15] The section on incomes covered income from pensions; this section will not go into more detail on pension wealth.

The level of older people's wealth depends on savings behaviour during their working lives: those with higher incomes and lower outgoings are most likely to put money into financial savings, mortgages and occupational or personal pensions.[16] Older people with high incomes tend to have high levels of wealth as well, but there are large variations within income groups.

Wealth is usually built up through working life, and so average wealth peaks around State Pension Age (SPA). Lump sums from occupational pension schemes will also contribute to a wealth peak around SPA. Figure 7.17 shows this pattern for net financial and physical wealth – although there are similar patterns for different forms of wealth.

Older age groups have less wealth than those around SPA. This is partly a cohort effect: each new generation tends to retire with more wealth than the last, as economic growth will normally increase their earnings and ability to save while they are in work. Older pensioners may also have used some of their wealth during retirement, and housing wealth will fall if pensioners move into smaller properties.

Figure **7.17**

Median net financial and physical wealth: by age, 2002

England

£ thousands

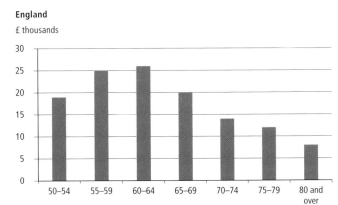

Source: English Longitudinal Study of Ageing, University College London

Wealth inequalities

There are large inequalities in the distribution of (non-pension) wealth, much larger than the inequalities for income. This is partly because there are no state benefits to ensure a minimum level of wealth as there is for income. Figure 7.18 shows the 25th percentile, median and 75th percentile for non-pension wealth (the total of financial, physical, and housing wealth) in 2002. The bottom quarter of older people have non-pension wealth of less than £25,000, whereas the top quarter has wealth of over £181,000.

The levels of inequality are greater for the financial wealth component; the bottom quarter of people aged 50 and over have less than £1,500 of financial wealth, whereas the top

Figure **7.18**

Total non-pension wealth[1] for people aged 50 and over, 2002

England

£ thousands

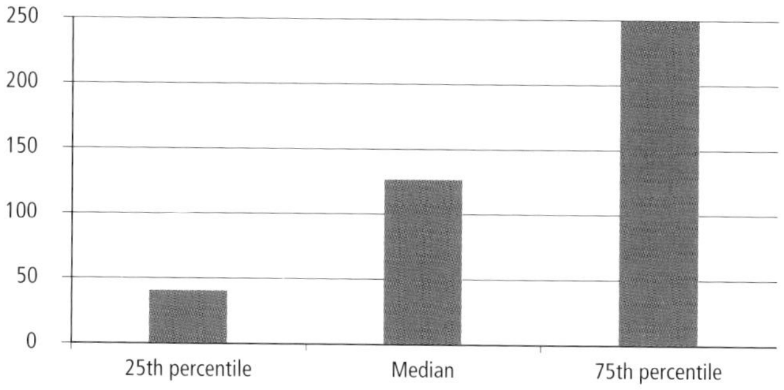

1 Non-pension wealth is defined as the total of financial, physical and housing wealth minus any debt.

Source: English Longitudinal Study of Ageing, University College London

Table **7.19**

Ownership of financial assets[1], 2002

England	Percentages
Savings and current account[2]	91
ISAs	43
TESSAs	16
Premium bonds	35
National Savings	7
PEPS	18
Shares	33
Trusts	10
Bonds	10
Other savings	11

1 Males and females aged 50 and over.
2 Includes interest-bearing deposit accounts and current accounts.

Source: English Longitudinal Study of Ageing, University College London

quarter have over £44,500. Housing wealth is more evenly spread: although 27 per cent of people aged 50 and over have no housing wealth (that is do not own their own home), the median housing wealth is £52,500 and a quarter of over 50s have over £100,000 of housing wealth. It should be noted that housing wealth is self reported, so will be subject to some misreporting.

Types of assets

Older people hold a range of assets. Table 7.19 shows the proportion of those aged 50 and over holding different types of financial assets: over 90 per cent of older people hold savings accounts of some form, and over 40 per cent have Individual Savings Accounts (ISAs). The proportion of older people with different types of assets varies with age: older pensioners are less likely to have most types of financial assets, other than savings accounts. There are some types of financial assets which see large differences in the level of ownership between different age groups, often reflecting when different savings products were introduced. Some products are only available to some age groups, for example Pensioners Guaranteed Income Bonds are only available to people over 60. Nearly half (47 per cent) of 50-54 year olds have ISAs, compared with 24 per cent of those over 80. The level of ownership of premium bonds falls from 38 per cent of 50–54 year olds to 28 per cent of the over 80 age group.

Housing makes up a large proportion of older people's wealth. Across all age groups the total value of fixed assets, such as houses and property, exceeds funds stored in more accessible forms such as savings accounts or investments.[17]

As with other forms of wealth, estimates show housing wealth is highest in the age groups just before State Pension Age. Within the over 50 age group, the oldest people (those aged 80 and over) are most likely to live in rented accommodation of some form (usually housing association or rented accommodation) and so have lower housing wealth: 17 per cent of men aged 60–64 are in rented accommodation compared with 29 per cent of men over 80. Single women have higher housing wealth than other pensioners, reflecting that they have often been left a family home on the death of their partner.

Wealth and health

The 2002 English Longitudinal Study of Ageing (ELSA) points to a strong relationship between self-reported health and the stock of wealth older people hold. Across all age groups, those reporting excellent or good health had two to three times the median wealth of those people who reported having only fair or poor health.

In all age groups, older people with less wealth are more likely to say they have poor or fair health (as opposed to good, very good, or excellent health). Thirty nine per cent of those aged 50–54 in the lowest wealth quintile reported poor or fair health, compared with 9 per cent of those in the highest wealth quintile (Figure 7.20 – see overleaf). The gap between the lowest and highest quintiles narrows in older age groups: 45 per cent of those aged 80 and over in the lowest wealth quintile reported poor or fair health, compared with 29 per cent of those in the highest wealth quintile.

Table **7.20**

People reporting poor or fair health: by wealth quintile[1] and age, 2002

England

Percentages

	50–54	55–59	60–64	65–69	70–74	75–79	80 and over
Lowest wealth quintile	39	45	45	44	49	50	45
Quintile 2	22	29	35	30	38	43	45
Quintile 3	15	20	24	21	29	30	43
Quintile 4	9	17	15	19	25	21	27
Highest wealth quintile	9	9	12	15	20	20	29

1 Wealth quintiles are defined within each five-year age group.

Source: English Longitudinal Study of Ageing, University College London

The stock of wealth an individual holds is also related to their expectations of how long they will live. Those in the highest wealth quintiles expected to live longer on average. ELSA asked respondents to report the average probability of living to an older age. The survey found that those aged under 65 in the richest wealth quintile reported an average probability of 69 per cent of living to age 75. Those in the poorest wealth quintile reported an average probability of 59 per cent of living to 75. The difference between the lowest and highest wealth quintiles was smaller for those at older ages.

Saving

The previous section has discussed older people's wealth. This section looks at the process of saving – that is putting aside current income for later use. People may build up wealth in a number of ways, including buying property, or investing in businesses. This section will focus on financial savings (for example through bank or building society accounts) and pension saving.

The section on pensioners incomes noted that people in employment, in good health, and in well paid jobs were most likely to build up rights to private pensions. The same factors also impact on how likely different people are to save, and so the same groups (women, ethnic minorities) are also unlikely to build up savings.

Research based on the British Household Panel Survey shows that people in their 40s and 50s are most likely to be saving.[18] The 40-49 year old age group is most likely to be saving for retirement, with 62 per cent saving, but this proportion falls with age: 52 per cent of 50-59 year olds and 12 per cent of 60-69 year olds were saving for retirement. The majority of people saving for retirement were doing so through an occupational pension scheme.

Other saving also falls as people get older, with retired people less likely to save than those in work (although with a smaller gap than might have been expected). Nearly half (46 per cent) of working-age people in 2000 were saving beyond their pension contributions, compared with 34 per cent of those of pensionable age. When they did save, working-age people put by an average of £128 a month compared with those of pensionable age who saved an average of £92 a month.

Older people save for a variety of reasons. Of those retired people who were saving, a large proportion said they were saving for holidays (22 per cent cited this as a reason) and many said they were saving for 'old age' (7 per cent).

Survey research carried out by the Joseph Rowntree Foundation suggests that some older people are also prompted to save by their desire to leave an inheritance or pass on something to their children or relatives.[19] This was greater among some ethnic minority groups - particularly among Asians who said they would be careful with their money in order to leave a bequest. The research also showed that although people like the idea of being able to leave a bequest, most do not think that older people should be careful with their money just so that they have something to bequeath. The majority of older people said they will enjoy life rather than worry about inheritance.

Debt

People in older age groups are less likely to have some form of debt than younger adults (Figure 7.21). This might be expected as people take out debt during their working life, paying it back before they retire from paid work. Over 19 per cent of those over 50 still have outstanding credit card debt once monthly balances have been paid, and 24 per cent have other kinds of outstanding debt. Levels of debt are greater among

Figure **7.21**

People with debt: by age and type of debt[1], 2002

England

Percentages

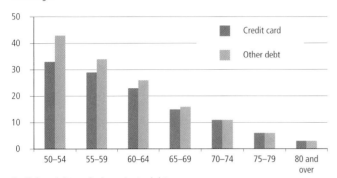

1   Other debt excludes private debt.

Source: English Longitudinal Study of Ageing, University College London

younger age groups: 33 per cent of those aged 50–54 have outstanding credit card debt compared with only 6 per cent for those aged 75–79.

The proportions of older people with debt are similar for both sexes: 21 per cent of men and 18 per cent of women have outstanding credit card debt.[20] Research for Age Concern and the Consumer Credit Counselling Service shows an increasing number of people in their 50s seeking help and advice on their debt problems over the five years since 1998.[21]

Expenditure patterns

Households headed by people in older age groups spend less on average than those in younger age groups. For households headed by someone aged 50–64 spending was £441 a week

Figure **7.22**

Household expenditure: by age of household reference person, 2003/04

United Kingdom

£ per week

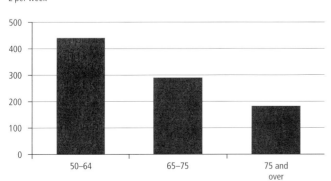

Source: Expenditure and Food Survey, Office for National Statistics

in 2003/04, while for households headed by someone aged over 75 weekly spending was an average of £183 (Figure 7.22). This lower level of spending partly reflects smaller household size: as people get older their children leave home, and the very old are more likely to be in single person households; in contrast younger households are more likely to have people in work. However, even after all these factors are taken into account, older people report that they spend less of their income than younger groups.

As people get older the absolute amount they spend falls for almost all categories of spending. Their spending patterns also change, with an increasing proportion of their spending going on necessities such as food and housing, and falling proportions of the spending going on transport, recreation and culture (Table 7.23). Changes in spending patterns for older people are linked to changes in lifestyle. Expenses related to being in work, for example travel to work costs, will end at retirement. The different spending patterns of older age groups also reflect the changing way older people spend their time (see Chapter 8: Lifestyles and leisure), with falling mobility changing the way they can spend their money.

Table **7.23**

Household expenditure[1] as a percentage of total expenditure: by age of household reference person, 2003/04

United Kingdom   Percentages

	50–59	60–69	70–79	80 and over
Food & non-alcoholic drinks	10	12	15	15
Alcoholic drinks, tobacco & narcotics	3	3	3	2
Clothing & footwear	4	5	4	3
Housing[2], fuel & power	9	9	12	15
Household goods & services	9	8	9	7
Health	1	2	3	2
Transport	15	14	10	12
Communication	2	2	3	3
Recreation & culture	14	16	14	13
Education	1	0	0	0
Restaurants & hotels	7	7	6	5
Miscellaneous goods & services	8	7	9	9
Other expenditure items	15	12	13	13

1 One and two person households only, based on weighted data.
2 Housing excludes mortgage interest payments and Council Tax.

Source: Expenditure and Food Survey, Office for National Statistics

Table **7.24**

Household expenditure[1] as a percentage of total expenditure where the age of household reference person is 50 and over: by sex, 2003/04

United Kingdom   Percentages

	Household reference person	
	Males	Females
Food & non-alcoholic drinks	11	14
Alcoholic drinks, tobacco & narcotics	4	3
Clothing & footwear	2	5
Housing[2], fuel & power	14	16
Household goods & services	5	9
Health	2	2
Transport	15	7
Communication	3	3
Recreation & culture	13	12
Education	1	0
Restaurants & hotels	8	5
Miscellaneous goods & services	9	9
Other expenditure items	13	13

1 One and two person households only, based on weighted data.
2 Housing excludes mortgage interest payments and Council Tax.

Source: Expenditure and Food Survey, Office for National Statistics

There are distinct differences in the spending patterns of single men and women, even after taking into account the older average age of women. Men spend a higher proportion of their income on restaurants and hotels, and a much higher proportion of their income on transport than women (Table 7.24). Women spend higher proportions of their income on food, clothes and household goods. This may partially reflect the higher average incomes of single men compared to single women.

Glossary

Income

This report uses a number of definitions of income:

Gross income is defined as income from all sources, including the following components:

- usual net earnings from employment;

- profit or loss from self-employment (losses are treated as a negative income);

- Income from private pensions;

- Social security benefits (including Housing Benefit, Social Fund, maternity, funeral and community care grants but excluding Social Fund loans).

Total income is equal to gross income plus tax credits. For older people, and especially pensioners, income from tax credits is very small, and so there is little difference between total income and gross income.

Net income (before housing costs) is equal to gross income less direct taxes, which include income tax, national insurance and council tax. Income is also net of contributions to private pensions, maintenance and child support payments, and parental contributions to students living away from home.

Net income (after housing costs) is derived by deducting a measure of housing costs from before housing costs income. The housing costs deducted include:

- rent (gross of housing benefit);

- water rates, community water charges and council water charges;

- mortgage interest payments (net of tax relief);

- structural insurance premiums (for owner occupiers);

- ground rent and service charges.

There is no 'best' way of measuring incomes when they are being used as a proxy for someone's standard of living. Measures of net income before and after housing costs both have their advantages. Measuring income before housing costs are deducted will better reflect the standards of living people achieve if they choose to pay more for better housing. Measuring income after housing costs are deducted better reflects income available if people cannot easily choose to move house and reduce their housing costs.

Equivalisation. The process by which household income is adjusted to account for variation in household size and composition. Equivalisation allows us to compare the incomes of, for example, a couple and a single person. Household incomes are divided by household equivalence factors, which vary according to the number of adults and the number and age of dependants in the household. The results can be sensitive to the exact equivalisation factors used. For more information see the DWP publication *Households Below Average Incomes*.

Levels of analysis

We look at income on a number of levels. Which one is more appropriate depends on how much you are interested in someone's personal income, and how much sharing takes place within a couple or a household.

Individual – mainly used to look at the different incomes that men and women are personally entitled to. Measures of income on an individual level exclude certain sources of income which cannot easy be assigned to one member in a couple. Excluded sources of income include: Housing Benefit, Council Tax Benefit, and the value of property income from letting.

Benefit unit, or pensioner unit – a single adult or a couple living as married and any dependent children. Income on sources of income for pensioners is often presented on a benefit unit level. Presenting information for single pensioners and pensioner couples avoids the assumptions inherent in equivalisation.

Household – a single person or a group of people living at the same address as their only or main residence, who either share one meal a day together or share the living accommodation. Income measured on the household level is normally equivalised, and is used to compare the incomes of pensioners and older people to incomes of people of younger ages.

Averages and distributions

Mean – often described as the average, found by adding up all the values in a group and dividing by the number of values.

Median – the value in a distribution which divides it into two halves, so half the population will have income above the median, and half below. The median is often more representative of the 'typical' income someone receives, where the mean may be skewed by a small number of people with very high incomes.

Quintiles – the quintiles of a distribution divide it into five equal sized parts. So, the bottom income quintile group will be the fifth of the population with the lowest income.

Sources of information

The majority of the information in this chapter is based on three sample surveys. These are all household surveys so the information only reflects the household population, not, for example, people in nursing homes.

The Family Resources Survey (FRS) asks about incomes and other circumstances of households. Data from the FRS is available from 1994/95, and so some of the comparisons over time are based on 9 years of change. It has a target sample of 29,000 households each year. From 2002/03 the FRS covered the whole of the United Kingdom, but the results presented in this chapter are for Great Britain only.

The Expenditure and Food Survey (EFS), formerly the Family Expenditure Survey (FES), asks respondents about their expenditure and income. This survey is used for analysis of expenditure, and provides data on income from before FRS became available. Responses from over 6,000 households across the United Kingdom are obtained.

The English Longitudinal Study of Ageing (ELSA) is a survey of people aged 50 and above in England which asks about a wide range of circumstances including income, wealth, and health. The first wave of ELSA took place in 2002, the second in 2004 (data from the second wave be available in the first half of 2006). Responses were obtained from 8,000 households.

References

1   Department for Work and Pensions, Income Related Benefits Estimates of Take-Up in 2002/03.

2   Talbot C, Adelman L & Lilly R. (2005) *Encouraging take-up: awareness of and attitudes to Pension Credit,* DWP Research Report 234. Corporate Document Services.

3   McConaghy M, Hill C, Kane C, Lader D, Costigan P & Thornby M. (2003) *Entitled but not claiming? Pensioners, the Minimum Income Guarantee and Pension Credit.* DWP Research Report **197**. Corporate Document Services.

4   Ginn J & Arber S (2000) 'Ethnic Inequality in Later Life: variation in financial circumstances by gender and ethnic group', *Education and Ageing,* Volume **15** (1).

5   Nesbitt S & Neary D (2001) *Ethnic minorities and their pensions decisions: a qualitative study of Pakistani, Bangladeshi and white men in Oldham,* Joseph Rowntree Foundation: York.

6   Humphrey A et al. (2003) *Factors affecting the labour market participation of older people,* DWP research report no **200**, Corporate Document Services, Leeds.

7   Smith S. (2004) Can the Retirement Consumption *Puzzle be Resolved?* Evidence from the UK Panel Data, Institute for Fiscal Studies Working Paper No. **04/07**.

8   Department for Work and Pensions (2005) *Low-Income Dynamics* 1991–2003.

9   Council of European Union (5 March 2004) *Joint report by the Commission and the Council on social inclusion*, Brussels 7101/04 http://europa.eu.int/comm/employment_social/soc-prot/soc-incl/final_joint_inclusion_report_2003_en.pdf

10   Whetstone M. (2002) Hard times. *A study of pensioner poverty.* Centre for Policy on Ageing/Nestle Family Monitor.

11   Costigan P, Finch H, Jackson B, Legard R & Ritchie J. (1999) *Overcoming barriers:* Older people and Income Support, DSS Research Report 100. Corporate Document Services.

12   Parry J, Vegeris S, Hudson M, Barnes H & Taylor R. (2004) *Independent living in later life.* Department for Work and Pensions Research Report **216**. Corporate Document Services.

13   Department for Work and Pensions (2003) *Factors affecting the labour market participation of older people.* DWP research report no **200**.

14   Finch H & Elam G (1995) *Managing Money in Later Life.* DSS Research Report No. 38. HMSO: London.

15   Banks J, Emmerson C & Tetlow G. (2005) *Estimating Pension Wealth of ELSA Respondents*, IFS Working Paper, WP **05/09** (www.ifs.org.uk/wps/wp0509.pdf).

16   Rowlinson K, Whyley C & Warren T. (1999) *Wealth in Britain: A lifecycle perspective.* London: Policy Studies Institute/Joseph Rowntree Foundation: York.

17   Pensions Commission (2004) Pensions: Challenges and Choices. The First Report of the Pensions Commission. The Stationery Office: London.

18   McKay S & Kempson E. (2003). *Savings and life events*, DWP Research Report Number **194**. Leeds: Corporate Document Services.

19   Rowlingson K & McKay S (2005) *Attitudes to Inheritance in Britain.* Bristol: The Policy Press.

20   Marmot M, Banks J, Blundell R, Lessof C & Nazroo J (eds) (2003) Health, *welfare and lifestyles of the older population in England: The 2002 English Longitudinal Study of Ageing.* London: IFS.

21   *Do We Have a Middle-Aged Debt Bulge?* An analysis prepared by Consumer Credit Counselling Service (CCCS) in conjunction with Age Concern (September 2004).

Further reading

Brewer M, Goodman A, Shaw J & Shepard A. (2005) *Poverty and Inequality in Britain: 2005.* IFS. www.ifs.org.uk/publications.php?publication_id=3328

Department for Work and Pensions (2003). *Measuring Child Poverty.* www.dwp.gov.uk/consultations/consult/2003/childpov/final.pdf

Department for Work and Pensions (2005). *A Guide to State Pensions.* www.thepensionservice.gov.uk/resourcecentre/np46/home.asp

Office for National Statistics (2005) *Pension Trends 2005.* Palgrave MacMillan: London. www.statistics.gov.uk

Piachaud D, Sutherland H, Sefton T. (2003) *Poverty in Britain: The Impact of Government Policy since 1997.* Joseph Rowntree Foundation.

Department for Work and Pensions (2004). *Opportunity for All*, Sixth Annual Report.

Lifestyles and leisure interests

A Soule

Department for Work and Pensions

Chapter 8

Key findings

- The increase in life expectancy over recent years has allowed people to enjoy more leisure time in later life. Older people take part in a range of leisure activities, both in and out of the home

- The nature of activities older people may choose to spend time on depends on their health, living arrangements and financial circumstances. The take up of leisure activities is generally lower for people in older age groups, due to declining health and mobility

- People's ability to travel affects their quality of life. Older people's travelling patterns depend in a large measure on their health and cognitive ability which is likely to be lower in older age groups. Car usage also declines with age

- Older people's lifestyles are also influenced by their desire to participate in society and develop themselves. Many older people actively involve themselves with clubs, societies and organisations, and also learn new skills

- Fear of crime can adversely affect older people's lifestyles and limit their social life. Fear of crime increases with age for both men and women. Women in all age groups were more fearful than men about being burgled, mugged or physically attacked

Introduction

The increase in life expectancy over the past century has meant that people now have a longer period of time in retirement than ever before. This chapter looks at the lifestyles of older people in the broad context of the time they spend on their leisure activities and the degree of their involvement with them. The leisure activities which people involve themselves with in later life are closely linked to their desire to retain independence.[1] For many older people, this means an ability to pursue activities which enable them to go out and socialise. For others, it means an ability to do things which form a part of their routine, such as gardening or watching television.

Participation levels generally decrease with age as they are affected by factors such as health, financial circumstances and individual aspirations. People in older age groups tend to have poorer health and have reduced incomes after retirement. Many people in their 50s have high disposable incomes as a result of paying off much of their mortgages, and with children leaving home. As people leave the labour market, they have more time to spend on leisure, but at this point their disposable income falls. Some people in older age groups will also experience declining health which leads to reduced participation in the leisure activities they had earlier engaged in.

This chapter will examine the *time* older people spend on various leisure activities as well the extent of their involvement in them. For ease of discussion, these activities are classed under three broad headings: *Staying in, Going out,* and *Participation in the wider community.*

Time spent on leisure activities

Older people below State Pension Age (SPA - 65 in men, 60 in women) are normally in work and therefore have less time for leisure activities than those who are retired. Family commitments also influence older people's use of their leisure time. For example, those older people with caring responsibilities for their spouses or family members would have less time for themselves.

The UK Time Use Survey 2000 suggests that the leisure choices of older people change as they get older. People in older age groups generally spend time on more sedate activities compared with those aged under 65. The time spent on watching TV, reading and listening to music increases substantially with age (Table 8.1). Conversely, the amount of time dedicated to more active pursuits, such as gardening or cultural and entertainment activities, falls in the 75 and over age group.

Table **8.1**

Time spent on selected activities[1]: by age, 2000

United Kingdom   Minutes per day

	50–64	65–74	75 and over
TV and video	149.96	189.53	203.20
Social life and entertainment & culture	60.14	65.50	59.53
Reading and listening to the radio/music	40.65	63.33	80.01
Resting	24.23	36.29	43.52
Food preparation	47.32	59.62	64.07
Cleaning and house repairs	34.73	38.30	36.52
Gardening or pets	28.09	33.07	21.33

1 Details of how people spend their time each day were recorded – adults aged 16 and over were asked to keep a detailed diary of how they spent their time on a selected day at the weekend.

Source: Time Use Survey, Office for National Statistics

People in older age groups are likely to find it difficult to take part in outdoor activities due to declining health and mobility as they get older. A significant proportion of their leisure time is therefore spent on activities in and around the home. People in older age groups spend more time resting at home during the day. Those aged over 75 spend an average of three quarters of an hour per day resting nearly 20 minutes more than that spent by 50–64 year olds. The over 50s also reported spending, in general, around half an hour per day on cleaning and house repairs. The amount of time spent on food also increases with age. People aged 65 and over spend more time on preparing food than those aged 50–64.

Staying in

Gardening and pets

Many older people spend time gardening and looking after pets. According to the British Household Panel Survey in 2002, around 42 per cent of those over the age of 50 did gardening at least once a week, which was more than double the proportion of those under the age of 50 (18 per cent).

People's decision to have pets or to garden will be affected by their health and the type of housing they have. Older people in poor health can find looking after a garden or a pet physically demanding. Some older people may also be living in accommodation which places restrictions on having a pet.

People in older age groups, especially those living on their own, are likely to feel isolated due to contracting social networks.[2] In many cases, having a pet can offset this feeling of isolation and lead to a greater feeling of security within their home.[3] People who are retired and are reasonably mobile are likely to spend more time with pets than those in younger age groups. The UK Time Use Survey 2000 found that those aged 60–74 spent more time with pets and walking the dog than those aged 50–59 and those over the age of 75.

Internet and mobile phones

Use of the Internet and mobile phones can help older people to remain independent by making it easier for them to communicate with their family and friends when they want to. These facilities can also help them in accessing many commercial and public services readily, for example, Internet shopping or having to call emergency services using mobile phones.

Being a relatively new technology, Internet usage is higher among the younger age groups (Figure 8.2). Men and women aged 50–54 have the highest Internet and email use (around 60 per cent for men and 48 per cent of women), in contrast to

Figure **8.2**

Use of Internet and mobile phone[1]: by age and sex, 2002

England

Percentages

a)   **Uses Internet**

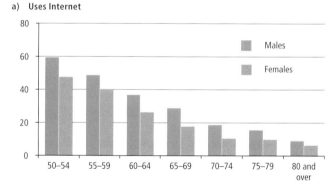

b)   **Owns a mobile phone**

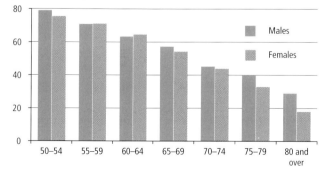

1   *Respondents asked whether they used Internet or email and if owned a mobile phone.*

Source: English Longitudinal Study of Ageing, University College London

those over 80 where only 9 per cent of men and 7 per cent of women use the Internet and email. Men in all age groups have a higher rate of Internet usage than women.

According to research by the Department for Work and Pensions, pensioners are generally more hesitant in their use of the Internet than those in working-age groups.[4] Those who have school and college qualifications are slightly more confident about using the Internet. The English Longitudinal Study of Ageing in 2002 showed that differences in the use of the Internet and email are also observed by occupational groups. For those aged 50–59, around 81 per cent of men and 70 per cent of women in the managerial and professional occupational group used the Internet and email compared with 30 per cent of men and 24 per cent of women in the routine and manual occupations.

The use of mobile phones is more prevalent than use of the Internet among older people. For those aged 80 and over, 29 per cent of men used mobile phones as opposed to 9 per cent of men who had Internet access. Trends are similar for women, with 18 per cent of those aged 80 or over using mobile phones as opposed to only 7 per cent having Internet access (Figure 8.2).

Older people may face certain barriers in using electronic services like costs or lack of knowledge or confidence in using computers. According to the National Statistics Omnibus Survey, people in older age groups are more likely to state they did not want, did not need, or had no interest in the Internet as their reason for non-use.

Going out

Travel

The ability to travel has a direct impact on older people's quality of life.[5] The National Statistics Omnibus Survey in 2001 found that those older people who had access to either a car or a van were more likely than those without to describe their quality of life as good or very good. The survey also found a positive correlation between access to transport and the frequency with which older people take part in social activities. Of those older people who took part in no social activities, only 37 per cent of them had access to a vehicle, while 85 per cent of those who took part in at least 6 activities per month had access to a car or van.

Car usage declines with age and varies by sex. Fewer older women than men have access to cars. According to the General Household Survey, in 2001, 77 per cent of men and 64 per cent of women aged 65–74 had access to a car. Among those aged 75 and over these proportions were far lower at 57 per cent and 34 per cent respectively.

A much greater proportion of older men than women held a full car driving licence – in 2003/04, 70 per cent of men in the 70 and over age group held a full driving licence in contrast to only 27 per cent of women of the same age (Figure 8.3). In the past, a greater proportion of men held driving licences than women. In the mid-1970s, 24 per cent of women aged 50–59 held a driving license compared with 75 per cent of men. The gender gap at older ages is expected to further reduce in the future as, in 2003/04, 70 per cent of 50–59 year old women held a driving licence compared with 91 per cent of men of the same age.

The English Longitudinal Study of Ageing showed that, in 2002, those in the older age groups were more likely to use public transport than those in younger age groups. Twenty three per cent of women aged 70–74 said they use public transport a lot, compared with 14 per cent of those aged 50–54. The study also showed that the most common reason for those who never or rarely used public transport was the lack of availability. Around 85 per cent of men and 83 per cent of women aged 50 and over said that they did not take public transport because it is not available.

Overall, people in younger age groups travel more than those in older age groups. According to the National Travel Survey,

Figure **8.3**

Full car driving license holders: by age and sex, 1975/76 and 2003/04

Great Britain

Percentages

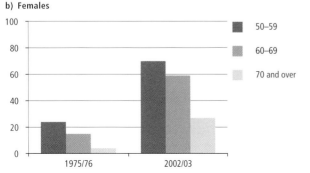

Source: National Travel Survey, Department for Transport

Figure **8.4**

Trips[1] per person per year: by age and sex, 2003/04

Great Britain

Numbers

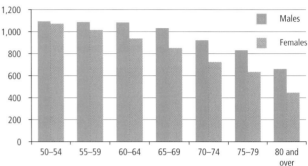

1　A trip is defined as a one-way course of travel having a single main purpose.

Source: National Travel Survey, Department for Transport

the number of trips (where 'trips' are defined as a one-way course of travel having a single main purpose) people in Great Britain make declines with age (Figure 8.4). During 2003/04, men and women aged 50–54 made an average of 1,094 and 1,074 trips respectively. This compares with 661 and 447 trips respectively for men and women aged 80 and over.

Travelling habits are significantly affected by work patterns, and retiring from work therefore has a considerable influence upon the travelling routines of older people. This is illustrated by the fact that in 2003/04 those aged 50-59 made around 300 trips for business or commuting purposes on average, while those aged 70 and over made hardly any. Shopping, personal business and leisure are the most common reasons for travel by older people. Health status and cognitive ability also have an impact on older people's travelling patterns. The ability to access local amenities like post offices or local shops is lower for older age groups.[6]

Older people also travel considerably less distance than those in younger age groups. In 2003/04, men aged 50-59 travelled 10,900 miles on average. This was more than double the 4,500 miles travelled by those aged 70 and over. Women in these age groups travelled around 7,100 miles and 3,100 miles respectively

Holidays

According to the 2002 English Longitudinal Study of Ageing, over half of people aged 50 and over in England had taken a holiday in the UK in the last 12 months. As a general trend, the proportion of older people taking a holiday decreases with age. As people get older, they become less inclined to travel abroad and instead choose more often to holiday in the UK.

Figure **8.5**

Holidays taken in the last twelve months: by age, 2002

England

Percentages

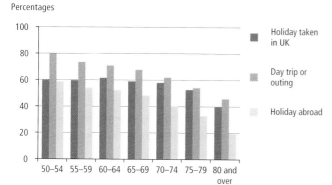

Source: English Longitudinal Study of Ageing, University College London

The number of people taking holidays abroad starts to decline among those aged 50 and over (Figure 8.5). The number of people holidaying in the UK remains broadly stable, until it too starts to decline among those aged 70 and over.

Sporting and physical activities

People who have been active during their working life are more likely to remain active after retirement.[7] The levels of participation in sporting and physical activities by older people depend to a large extent on their interest and involvement when they were younger. Older people also derive direct physical benefits from participating in these activities. These include improved and increased balance, strength, coordination, flexibility and endurance.[8]

Participation in sport decreases with age. In 2002/03, 60 per cent of people aged 45–59 had taken part in sport or physical activity – twice the proportion of those who participated in the

Figure **8.6**

Participation in one sport or physical activity in the last four weeks before interview: by age, 2002/03

Great Britain

Percentages

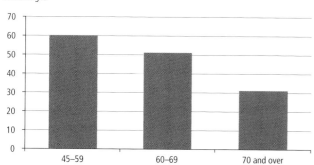

Source: General Household Survey, Office for National Statistics

70 and over age group (Figure 8.6). This drop in participation may be due to the lower health and mobility status of older age groups (see chapters 5 and 6 for a detailed discussion on health issues affecting older people).

The highest level of participation was in walking, although participation levels declined with age: 40 per cent of those aged 45-59 had walked two miles or more at one stretch for recreational purposes in the four weeks before the survey as opposed to only 22 per cent of people over 70 (Table 8.7). About 4 per cent of people aged 70 and over had also taken part in keep fit activities and 3 per cent had swum.

Table **8.7**

Participation[1] in a sport, game or physical activity: by age, 2002/03

Great Britain

Percentages

	45–59	60–69	70 and over
Walking[2]	40	37	22
Swimming	13	7	3
Keep fit	11	7	4
Cycling	8	4	2
Snooker/pool/billiards	5	3	2
Golf	5	4	2
Weight training	3	1	0
Running	3	1	0
Fishing	2	2	0

1 Participating in the four weeks before interview.
2 Two miles or more for recreational purposes.

Source: General Household Survey, Office for National Statistics

Attendance at arts and cultural events

Older people take part in a variety of arts and cultural activities. An Arts Council study showed that in 2003, people aged 55–64 were more likely than other older age groups to have gone to musicals, craft exhibitions, visual arts exhibitions, classical music and opera.[9] Those aged 65 and over were the least likely to attend films, live dance events, cultural festivals, events connected with books or writing, and video or electronic art events. The study also showed some differences in attendance patterns between men and women. For example, women were more likely to attend craft exhibitions than men. However, for all activities, the proportions attending decrease in older age groups. In 2003, 84 per cent of those aged 45–54 attended at least one event in the last 12 months falling to 47 per cent of those aged 75 and over (Figure 8.8 – see overleaf).

Older people from ethnic minorities mainly attend arts events which relate to their own cultural heritage rather than mainstream arts.[10] Another study for the Arts Council suggests

Figure **8.8**

Attendance at arts activities[1] in last 12 months: by age, 2003

England

Percentages

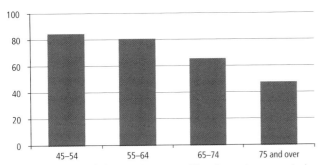

1 Arts activities include attending events like: play or drama, musical, art, photography or sculpture exhibition, craft exhibition, pantomime, classical music, opera or operetta, jazz concert, visit to a stately home/castle and a visit to a well known park or garden.

Source: Arts Council of England

Figure **8.9**

Frequency of contact with relatives, friends or neighbours for people aged 65 and over, 2001/02

Great Britain

Percentages

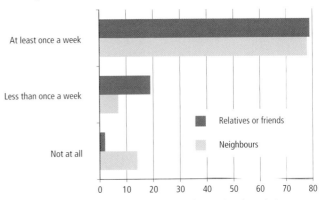

Source: General Household Survey, Office for National Statistics

that some minority groups, particularly Asian communities, feel a deep commitment to pass on their cultural heritage to their children through participation and involvement in arts events. Arts and cultural activities were viewed as occasions which brought various community groups together across the generations.

Older people face a variety of barriers to attendance at arts and cultural activities. In the 2001 National Statistics Omnibus Survey, poor health and lack of transport were given as major reasons for not attending these activities in older age groups, particularly among those aged 75 and over. Generally younger people were more likely than older respondents to cite cost as a reason for not attending.

Social networks and community participation

Older people place a great value upon social relationships and friendships.[11] Where they exist, such social relationships can also contribute to better health for older people. Furthermore, because older people travel less, social networks tend to be closely linked to where they live.

Family support and social networks

Families continue to remain the main support for older people in times of hardship or grief. This is true even in cases where older people live away from their families and where there may be periods when contact is not always kept up between family members. In 2001/02, 79 per cent of people aged 65 and over living in households in Great Britain saw a relative or friend at least once a week (Figure 8.9). Only a small minority (2 per cent) did not see relatives or friends at all.

The frequency of contact is linked to whether older people live alone or in a couple, particularly among the very old. Among those aged 75 and over, 82 per cent of those who lived alone saw relatives or friends at least once a week, compared with 73 per cent of those who lived in a couple.[12]

Seventy eight per cent of people aged 65 and over said they had contact with neighbours at least once a week, while 14 per cent had no contact at all. Contact with neighbours tends to decrease with age: 81 per cent of 65–69 year olds had weekly contact, compared with 71 per cent of those aged 85 and over. Research also shows that for older people from ethnic minorities, family members tend to live close to each other, and often several generations may share living arrangements.[13,14]

Membership of organisations

The majority of older people belong to at least one organisation. Overall the likelihood of being a member of an organisation falls with older age. According to the English Longitudinal Study of Ageing in 2002, 32 per cent of men and 38 per cent of women aged 50–54 were not a member of an organisation, compared with 50 per cent of men and 51 per cent of women over 80.

Membership of different types of organisation varies with age – but not always in the same way. There are some organisations – such as sports clubs – where membership falls with age, and other organisations – such as church and other religious groups – where membership is highest for the oldest age groups. With some groups, such as evening classes, membership increases up to around State Pension Age and declines afterwards.

The chance of being a member of an organisation is generally higher for those in the higher socio-economic groups: for example those in the managerial and professional groups were almost twice as likely to be in tenants' groups, residents' groups and neighbourhood watch groups as people from the routine and manual socio-economic groups (26 per cent compared with 14 per cent).

Membership of organisations is generally lower for those who report their health to be fair or poor: 28 per cent of men in excellent or very good health were members of a charitable association compared with 11 per cent of men in fair or poor health (see Chapter 5 for more information).

There are differences in membership levels between men and women – with men being more likely to be members of political parties, and social clubs, whereas women are more likely to be members of churches or charitable organisations (Figure 8.10).

For both men and women, membership of a religious organisation forms a big part of their overall involvement with organisations and societies. Although membership of religious organisations increases with age, there are differences between the membership levels of men and women. Women at older ages were more likely than men to take part in religious activities: 36 per cent of women aged 80 and over were members of a religious organisation as opposed to 23 per cent of men of the same age.

Voluntary activities

Older people participate in communities in different ways and many of them choose to do so through volunteering. Many older people find that volunteering offers a means of making a meaningful contribution to society once the opportunity to do so through paid work has ceased.[15] For some older people, volunteering may be a continuation of activities in which they participated during their working lives, while others may see retirement as an opportunity for taking up a variety of activities for the first time. The benefits which people derive from voluntary work include keeping physically and mentally fit, a sense of purpose and personal fulfilment.[16]

Older people may choose to volunteer in a formal way, with charities or groups, or they may take up informal volunteering by helping friends or neighbours. The proportions of older people who take on informal volunteering in all age groups over 50 are higher than those who choose to take up formal volunteering.

In 2003, 33 and 29 per cent of people aged 50–64 volunteered informally and formally respectively (Table 8.11). People aged 65–74 have the highest levels of informal volunteering - 39 per cent in 2003. People within this age group are most likely to have retired from paid work, and so have more available time, while those in the older age group are more likely to have health problems or reduced mobility which prevents them volunteering.

Figure **8.10**

Involvement in organisations for people aged 50 and over: by sex, 2002

England

Percentages

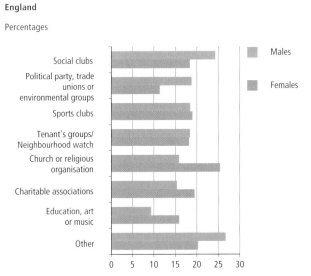

Source: English Longitudinal Study of Ageing, University College London

Table **8.11**

People participating[1] in voluntary and community activities: by age, 2001 and 2003

England   Percentages

	2001	2003
Informal volunteering[2]		
50–64	31	33
65–74	36	39
75 and over	27	32
Formal volunteering[3]		
50–64	28	29
65–74	28	30
75 and over	19	19

1 Participating at least once a month in the twelve months before interview.
2 Informal volunteering takes into account giving unpaid help to an individual or others who are not members of the family.
3 Formal volunteering includes giving unpaid help through groups, clubs or organisations.

Source: Citizenship Survey, Home Office

Civic participation and political awareness

Older people are more interested in politics than younger people. In a recent poll by MORI, 65 per cent of people over 55 claimed to be interested in politics, compared with 48 per cent of those under 35.[17] The likelihood of voting also rises with age.

Those in the oldest age groups are more likely to vote than those in the younger age groups (Table 8.12). In the 2001 General Election, 89 per cent of men and 81 per cent of women aged over 80 voted compared with 79 per cent of men and 77 per cent of women aged 50–54 years.[18] Older people are also more likely to be interested in local issues than younger people, demonstrated by their greater likelihood to vote in local elections. In 2003, 49 per cent of people over the age of 55 voted in the local elections compared with an overall turnout of 35 per cent.

Table 8.12

People who voted in 2001 General Election: by sex and age, 2002

England   Percentages

	Males	Females
50–54	79	77
55–59	82	78
60–64	82	84
65–69	85	86
70–74	89	82
75–79	89	87
80 and over	89	81

Source: English Longitudinal Study of Ageing, University College London

The level of newspaper readership also suggests people's awareness of national and local affairs. According to the 2002 English Longitudinal Study of Ageing, the readership of newspapers among men was highest among those in their 70s. For women, those in their 60s and late 70s reported the highest rates of daily newspaper readership. For both men and women, those in their 50s reported the lowest rates of daily newspaper readership.[18]

Many older people also make use of public libraries for reading for pleasure, getting information or learning. In 2004 approximately 149 million visits to libraries per year were made by people over 55, and around 30 per cent of library users were over the age of 65.[19] Apart from borrowing books, older people also make use of other facilities offered by most public libraries – for example access to daily newspapers, use of computer and Internet facilities.

Older learners: education and training

Many older people continue to participate in learning new skills even after they have retired from active employment. The National Adult Learning Survey (NALS) carried out by the Department for Education and Skills shows that over the last few years, there has been a general increase in learning participation among older people across all age groups (over 50). Table 8.13 shows that between 1997 and 2002, the increase was highest (7 percentage points) for those aged 50–59. There was a smaller increase (4 percentage points) for those aged 60–69.

Table 8.13

People reporting some learning[1]: by age

England and Wales   Percentages

	50–59	60–69	70 and over
1997	67	47	..
2001	74	49	25
2002	74	51	28

1 Data not collected for 70 and over in 1997.

Source: National Adult Learning Survey, Department for Education and Skills

People aged 50–59 were more likely to take part in vocational learning than those in older age groups (70 and over). Two thirds of those aged 50–59 years old took part in vocational learning compared with 6 per cent of those 70 and over.

The National Adult Learning Survey 2002 also asked non-learners (those that had not participated in any form of learning in the last three years) whether they would have liked to have done some learning. Table 8.14 shows a clear age pattern: non-learners at younger ages were more likely to say that they would have liked to have done some learning, while older non-learners were much less likely to be interested.

Computing and leisure studies were popular choices among older non-learners who would have liked to have done some

Table 8.14

Whether older non-learners would like to have done some learning, 2002

England and Wales   Percentages

	50–59	60–69	70 and over
Yes definitely	13	10	6
Yes maybe	20	21	11
No	66	69	83

Source: National Adult Learning Survey, Department for Education and Skills

learning (Table 8.15). A relatively large proportion of older non-learners wanted to learn these subjects even at older age groups: 30 per cent of those aged 70 and over would have preferred to learn computing and 33 per cent leisure studies. A smaller proportion of older people also wanted to take up professional training. This was observed more for those who were below the age of 70.

Table **8.15**

Non-learners preferred learning activities: by age, 2002

England and Wales   Percentages

	50–59	60–69	70 and over
Computing	33	29	30
Leisure activities	20	27	33
Professional training	13	10	3
Academic	5	9	7
English/writing skills	3	4	4
Basic skills	2	3	1
Self-development	2	1	2
Driving lessons	1	2	2

Source: National Adult Learning Survey, Department for Education and Skills

Despite the positive trend of increasing learning participation among older people, the barriers they face are much like those faced by people in younger age groups. For example, those with no or low qualifications are much less likely to take up learning. Older learners are more likely to have no or low qualifications (36 per cent of those aged 30-39 years old have level one or no qualifications compared with 75 per cent of those aged 70 and over).[20]

Research by the Department for Education and Skills shows that informal non-accredited Adult and Community Learning, such as that delivered by a Local Education Authority (LEA), is especially popular with older people.[21] Over half of all learners studying on LEA adult education courses were aged 55 and over, and over a third were retired. For all those aged 55 and over, learning activity was higher for women. The benefits of this type of learning were almost wholly seen as personal rather than vocationally related. Older learners were likely to say that learning had a positive effect on their physical, mental and emotional well being. Learning also had a positive impact on older people's social lives, something reported by 50 per cent of those aged 65 and over. Men aged 55 and over felt that learning had a positive effect on their family relationships.

Fear of crime and personal safety

Fear of crime does not refer to a particular incident, instead it refers to ways of thinking, feeling and acting that are more universal and somewhat more difficult to qualify. The perceived risk of crime can have a large effect on an individual's lifestyle, as it can lead to individuals changing their behaviour and limit their social activities.[22]

In 2003/04 people over the age of 60 in England and Wales were less worried about almost all crimes than people aged 30–59 except for being mugged (Table 8.16). A higher proportion of women aged 60 and over than men were worried about all types of crime examined in the British Crime Survey 2003/04.[23] The key areas of fear for older women (aged 60 and over) were physical attack, mugging and burglary. Older people felt more unsafe while walking alone in the dark than younger people. The proportion of women aged over 60

Table **8.16**

Worry about crime[1]: by sex and age, 2003/04

England and Wales   Percentages

	Burglary	Mugging	Physical attack	Rape	Insulted or pestered	Theft of a car	Theft from a car
Males							
30–59	11	6	5	3	4	14	14
60 and over	10	7	5	2	3	11	9
Females							
30–59	15	14	17	19	10	15	11
60 and over	14	15	13	12	7	12	8

1 *Percentage of people who were 'very worried' about selected types of crime.*

Source: British Crime Survey, Home Office

520554

feeling unsafe when walking alone in the dark was more than three times that of men – 29 per cent compared with 8 per cent respectively.

According to research conducted for the Home Office, a substantial proportion of older burglary victims were declining in health or had died, compared with the non-burgled sample.[24] This was despite the fact that people over the age of 60 are less at risk of burglary than those in younger age groups. In the study carried out on 56 burglary victims, 11 had died soon after, and a further nine had gone into residential care at the time of interview. In effect, those burgled were twice as likely to have died or to be in residential care than their non-burgled neighbours.

References

1   Secker J, Hill R, Villeneau L & Parkman S. (2003) Promoting independence: but promoting what and how? *Ageing and Society* **23(3)**: 375–391.

2   Phillipson C & Scharf T. (2004) *The Impact of Government Policy on Social Exclusion of Older People: A Review of the Literature.* London, Stationery Office, Social Exclusion Unit, Office of the Deputy Prime Minister.

3   Hart LA. (1995) The role of pets in enhancing human well-being: Effects for older people. In Robinson J (ed): *The Waltham Book of Human-Animal Interaction: Benefits and Responsibilities of Pet Ownership.* Pergamon/Elsevier.

4   Coleman N, Jeawody F & Wapshot J. (2002) *Electronic Government at the Department for Work and Pensions.* Department for Work and Pensions, Summary of Research Report No. **176**.

5   Banister D & Bowling A. (2004) Quality of life for the elderly: the transport dimension. *Transport Policy* **11(2)**: 105–115.

6   Marmot M, Banks J, Blundell R, Lessof C & Nazroo J (eds) (2003) *Health, welfare and lifestyles of the older population in England: The 2002 English Longitudinal Study of Ageing.* London: IFS.

7   Casey B. (2004) *Why are older people not more "active"?* Discussion paper pi-0408, Pensions Policy Institute, May 2004 http://www.pensions-institute.org/workingpapers/wp0408/pdf

8   *Health Benefits of Physical Activity,* Postnote, October 2001 Number **162**, Parliamentary Office of Science and Technology http://www.parliament.uk/post/pn162.pdf

9   Fenn C, Bridgewood A, Dust K, Hutton L, Jobson M & Skinner M. (2003) *Arts in England: Attendance, participation and attitudes in 2003,* Arts Council of England.

10   Jermyn H & Desai P. (2000) *What's in a Word? Ethnic minorities and the Arts.* Arts Council England.

11   Godfrey M, Townsend J & Denby T. (2004) *Building a good life for older people in local communities: The experience of ageing in time and place.* Joseph Rowntree Foundation: York.

12   Office for National Statistics. (2002) *Living in Britain.* Results from the 2001 General Household Survey. The Stationery Office: London.

13   Age Concern England (2002). *Black and Minority Ethnic Elders' issues.* Policy Unit, Age Concern England.

14   Beishon S, Madood T & Virdee S. (1998) *Ethnic Minority Families.* Policy Studies Institute, University of Westminster, London.

15   Smith JD & Gay P (2005). *Active ageing in active communities: volunteering and the transition to retirement.* Policy Press: Bristol.

16   Barnes H, Parry J & Lakey J. (2002) *Forging a New Future: the experiences and expectations of people leaving paid work over 50.* Bristol: Policy Press.

17   MORI report for the Electoral Commission. (2003) *Attitudes towards Voting and the Political Process.* http://www.mori.com/polls/2003/pdf/electoralcommission2.pdf

18   Hyde M & Janevic M (2003). Social activity. In (eds) M Marmot, J Banks, R Blundell, C Lessof, J Nazroo. *Health, wealth and lifestyles of the older population in England: the 2002 English Longitudinal Study of Ageing.* Institute for Fiscal Studies. London. Table 5A.**21**, p 202.

19   Chartered Institute of Public Finance and Accounting (2004) *Public Library User Survey.*

20   National Adult Learning Survey (2002/2003) Department for Education and Skills.

21   Morrell J, Chowdhury R & Savage B. (2004) *Progression from Adult and Community Learning.* Department for Education and Skills (Research report RR546) http://www.dfes.gov.uk/research/data/uploadfiles/rr546.pdf

22   McKee K (2000) Health, Fear of Crime and Psychosocial Functioning in Older People. *Journal of Health Psychology,* **5(4)**: 473–486.

23   Crime in England and Wales. (2003) *British Crime Survey Home Office Statistical Bulletin* 2002/2003, p.143, http://www.homeoffice.gov.uk/rds/pdfs2/hosb703.pdf

24   Donaldson R. (2003) Experiences of older burglary victims. *Home Office Findings* No.198. Home Office: London.